The SYBEX Prompter Series

HARD DISK INSTANT REFERENCE

The SYBEX Prompter Series

We've designed the SYBEX Prompter Series to meet the evolving needs of software users, who want essential information presented in an accessible format. Our best authors have distilled their expertise into compact *Instant Reference* books you can use to look up the precise use of any command—its syntax, available options, and operation. More than just summaries, these books also provide realistic examples and insights into effective usage drawn from our authors' wealth of experience.

The SYBEX Prompter Series also includes these titles:

Lotus 1-2-3 Instant Reference
Greg Harvey and Kay Yarborough Nelson

WordPerfect Instant Reference
Greg Harvey and Kay Yarborough Nelson

WordPerfect 5 Instant Reference
Greg Harvey and Kay Yarborough Nelson

dBASE Instant Reference
Alan Simpson

Turbo BASIC Instant Reference
Douglas Hergert

DOS Instant Reference
Greg Harvey and Kay Yarborough Nelson

HyperTalk Instant Reference
Greg Harvey

WordStar Instant Reference
David J. Clark

Ventura Instant Reference
Matthew Holtz

The SYBEX Prompter™ Series

HARD DISK INSTANT REFERENCE

Judd Robbins

San Francisco • Paris • Düsseldorf • London

The SYBEX Prompter Series
Editor in Chief: Rudolph S. Langer
Managing Editor: Barbara Gordon
Series Editor: James A. Compton
Editor: Michael Wolk

Cover design by Thomas Ingalls + Associates
Series book design by Ingrid Owen
Screen reproductions produced with Xenofont

Library of Congress Card Number: 88-63705
ISBN 0-89588-587-5
Manufactured in the United States of America
10 9 8 7 6 5 4 3 2 1

To the Zen of Writing

Acknowledgments

Once again, many people at SYBEX deserve credit for ensuring the high quality of this book. Unfortunately, only one name goes on the book jacket, while many names are deserving of recognition. The people who contributed their time, energy, and care to the development of this book are: Jim Compton, developmental editor; Michael L. Wolk, editor; Mark Taber, technical editor; Ingrid Owen, book design; Bob Myren and Jocelyn Reynolds, word processing; Winnie Kelly, typesetting; Ed Lin, proofreading; and Eleanor Ramos, paste-up.

At IBM, Scott Brooks was instrumental in making a copy of DOS 4 available for this project.

Table of Contents

Introduction

This book is based on one simple premise: quick access to information about using DOS (and other software) to manage the information stored on your hard disk. At times you may be uncertain about the meaning of a system message, or you may need to review the syntax of a particular hard-disk management command, or a disk operation may not produce the results you expect. You may simply want a quick definition of a key computer term.

The *Hard Disk Instant Reference* is intended to supply those answers and more. As a concise reference guide to a subject of increasing importance to personal computer users, this book brings together materials from diverse sources. The basic commands affecting your hard disk are here; so are the most advanced commands. All possible switches that affect the operation of those commands are also detailed, and the most important are illustrated with examples.

Besides command definitions, you'll find information on using third-party utilities, an extensive glossary, a guide to relevant error messages, troubleshooting tips, and complete partitioning information. In short, this book will help you achieve the maximum possible benefit from your hard disk system.

How the Book Is Organized

This *Instant Reference* is divided into three parts, which you can consult according to your needs. Ample cross-referencing will help you find sidelights and related information for almost any topic you look up.

Part I presents reference entries on the DOS commands used in hard disk management.

Chapter 1, "*Directory Management Commands,*" concentrates on those DOS commands that provide you with total control over the creation and manipulation of your directory trees. Chapter 2, "*File Management Commands,*" focuses similarly on the DOS commands that directly affect access to all disk files, whether they contain executable programs or data. Chapter 3, "*Hard-Disk Configuration Commands,*" brings together the various configuration commands that can play such an important role in helping you to establish and maintain a powerful and efficient implementation of DOS on your hard disks.

All three chapters are organized similarly. Each command is available at a glance, presented alphabetically for quick retrieval. The details you require appear in the following compact format:

Part II makes a bold statement about third-party utilities. From the thousands of utilities available to enhance your DOS system I've selected three excellent representatives, which provide significant value when you want to go beyond DOS and its hard disk commands. Chapter 4, "*Managing Your Disk Contents with the Norton Utilities*," describes the many useful, and sometimes essential, utilities included in the Norton Utilities. They are a major asset for more effectively managing both the data in files, and the detailed information about those files stored in your hard disk.

Chapter 5, "*Improving Your Hard-Disk Management with Q-DOS II*," discusses another DOS shell program offering alternative implementations for some DOS commands, while going beyond DOS in some ways. Available for use in both DOS 4 and earlier versions, Q-DOS II represents quite well the class of DOS hard-disk management programs whose interfaces are designed to be easy to learn and use.

Chapter 6, "*Making Backup Copies with Back-It*," introduces a replacement program for the DOS commands of BACKUP and RESTORE. Much more powerful, Back-It is strongly recommended as a means of improving the relatively meager capabilities of the DOS commands.

Part III consists of four appendices that present valuable hard-disk reference information. Appendix A is a glossary of all relevant hard-disk computer terms. Appendix B explains both cause and cure for DOS's various hard disk error and information messages. Appendix C offers a unique explanation of the typical hard disk problems that occur on your system, and a conceptual explanation of how to begin to fix those problems. Lastly, Appendix D provides a step-by-step procedure for partitioning your hard disk, a necessary stage in preparing it for use by DOS. This step is often taken only once, but without it you can't use your hard disk at all.

COMMAND NAME

The main heading is followed by a capsule definition of the command.

VERSION

The version of DOS in which the command first appeared and the version, if any, in which it was most recently enhanced.

SYNTAX

COMMAND[*parameters and switches*]

The notation used here is quite simple. The command word always appears in boldface regular type, as do any elements to be typed in literally as shown, such as the switches used with many commands. Placeholders for filenames and parameters whose values depend on context appear in lighter italic type. All optional elements are enclosed in square brackets. Alternatives, such as ON | OFF, are separated by a vertical bar. Following the syntax line each parameter is explained individually.

TYPE

Whether the command is internal (loaded into memory when DOS first starts up) or external (stored on disk until called up by name).

USAGE

A brief discussion of how the command is most commonly and effectively used.

RESTRICTIONS

Any limitations on the use of the command.

EXAMPLES

One or more illustrations of the command in use.

SEE ALSO

Entries to consult for related information.

User input appears in boldface type; DOS prompts and other screen displays are set in a lighter type.

Figure I.1: The format of a reference entry

Part I

Managing Your Hard Disk with DOS

DOS includes scores of unique commands that enable you to take complete charge of your operating system. Over half of these are important for the organization and management of your hard-disk system. This Part is arranged into three separate alphabetical groupings of commands. All those DOS commands having to do with the management of directories are presented in Chapter 1, while the remaining hard-disk commands designed to assist you in the manipulation of hard disk files are grouped into Chapter 2. Chapter 3 discusses those commands used to configure your hard disk.

Chapter 1

Directory Management Commands

All information stored on a DOS system can be found in one or more disk files. All files are stored in areas of a disk called directories. You can create these meaningful groupings of files and manipulate them to form useful and well-organized structures. DOS has various commands that specifically enable you to create, delete, discover, and modify directories. In addition, some commands allow you to control entire disks at once. This chapter concentrates on the DOS commands responsible for disk and directory management.

APPEND

The APPEND command causes the computer to search a predetermined set of directories for files with extensions other than .COM, .BAT, and .EXE.

VERSION

Introduced in MS-DOS 3.2 and PC-DOS 3.3; most recently enhanced in DOS 4.0

SYNTAX

[*d:path*]**APPEND**[*d1:path1*][;*d2:path2*...]
[/X[:OFF | ON]][/PATH:ON | OFF][/E][;]

d:path	represents the drive and path where the command file is located if it is not in the current directory. Unnecessary after the first time that APPEND is loaded, because it then becomes an internal command.
d1:path1	represents the first drive and directory searched after the default drive and directory.
d2:path2...	represents the second drive and directory searched after the default drive and directory, and so on.
/X or /X:ON	causes APPEND to act like the PATH command, searching for executable files (.COM, .EXE, .BAT) along the APPEND directory list.
/X:OFF	turns off the search feature for executable file extensions. Only files with extensions other than COM, EXE, or BAT are then found.

/PATH:ON	forces APPEND to search along its directory list for specified filenames, regardless of whether the indicated files have drive or path prefixes.
/PATH:OFF	directs APPEND to search for files only when you have omitted a drive or path prefix.
/E	stores the paths in the DOS environment, so that they can be changed with the SET command.
;	separates APPEND paths; used alone nullifies the APPEND command by erasing the path list.

TYPE

External upon first execution; internal after first execution. Conventionally, this type of command is called an external, terminate-and-stay-resident (TSR) program. It resides on disk until it is needed, thereby taking up no room in memory. When it is invoked for the first time, it comes into memory. When it has finished executing, however, it does not free the memory space it used. Instead it stays resident in memory, continuing to provide service.

USAGE

The two most common uses of APPEND are to allow DOS to locate overlay files for sophisticated application programs and to allow DOS to locate data files for referencing by those programs. These types of files (.OVL, .DTA, and so on) cannot be located by using the PATH command. Earlier versions of DOS could not find these support files easily unless they appeared in the current default directory.

The APPEND command tells DOS to open files to read from or write to. In earlier versions of DOS, you must use the PATH command to find executable files with .COM, .EXE, or .BAT extensions. The /X switch provides the ability to search for these executable files as well, effectively replacing the functionality of the PATH command.

Secondary processors come into being only when the COMMAND command is used in DOS. Within the framework of your DOS, COMMAND provides, among other things, the opportunity to run DOS from within application programs. The /E switch enables you to store APPEND path-name entries in the environment and to use the SET command while a secondary command processor is active. The new copy of the DOS environment that is passed to a secondary command processor will receive the initial directory list set into the APPEND string. Since these path values are stored in memory, they will be lost when the secondary command processor terminates (with the EXIT command) and returns control to the application program that invoked it.

RESTRICTIONS

DOS provides a default 128 bytes of memory in which to specify paths. Do not use this command in conjunction with the APPEND command in the IBM PC Network program or in the IBM PC LAN program.

Unless you specify otherwise, applications that use APPEND to locate files in various disk directories may save modified files in the default directory, which is sometimes not the directory they were called from. For example, suppose you edit a file with DOS's line editor, EDLIN. Suppose further that the file to be edited is not in the current directory, but is specified in the APPEND path list of directories. If you call the file (say TEST.TXT) by its name only—for example

EDLIN TEST.TXT

the edited version of the file will be saved in your current default directory. Clearly, this is a potentially deceptive aspect of APPEND's operation. The solution to this problem is to specify a full path name when referencing the file—for example

EDLIN \FW\DATA\TEST.TXT

When the edited file is eventually saved, it will be saved correctly in the original directory, not in the current directory.

EXAMPLES

Suppose you want to execute a simple batch file you wrote for a menu-management system. You want the file to reference and execute your database program in the DBMS directory, your computer-aided design program in the CAD directory, and your word processing program in the WP directory. You must enter the following command, which explicitly specifies that the DBMS and the WP directories are on drive C and the CAD directory is on drive D:

APPEND C:\DBMS;D:\CAD;C:\WP

This example assumes that any referenced data files also appear in those directories; if, in fact, any data files are located in subdirectories, you must add those subdirectory names to the APPEND path list.

Clearing the current path list for the APPEND command is one way to force DOS to limit its search to only the current working directory.

You can add an /X switch to this preceding command, and you will have the equivalent of a PATH command as well as an APPEND command. The same sequence of DBMS, CAD, and WP directories will be searched for all filenames, both executable and data types.

The APPEND command is also useful in a network environment to locate data files residing on computers other than your own (on other nodes on the network).

SEE ALSO

PATH

ASSIGN

ASSIGN redefines the actual drive identifier that handles specific disk requests.

VERSION

Introduced in PC-DOS 2.0 and MS-DOS 3.0

SYNTAX

[*d:path*]**ASSIGN** [*drive1* = *bigdrive1*] [*drive2* = *bigdrive2*] [...]

d:path	represents the drive and path where the command file is located if it is not in the current directory.
drive1	represents the original drive to be rerouted.
bigdrive1	represents the drive assigned to handle all of *drive1*'s requests.
drive2, *bigdrive2*,...	represents drives used for other assignments.

TYPE

External.

USAGE

Use the ASSIGN command for specialized redirection of file requests. The parameter list allows you to assign drive references from one drive to another. With no parameters, ASSIGN cancels all current assignments.

ASSIGN is used most frequently to run older applications that are restricted to specific drives, typically A or B diskette drives. Because practical use of DOS requires a hard disk, the most convenient use of an older program is to place both program and data files in a hard-disk directory or directories. This command makes that feasible.

RESTRICTIONS

Do not use ASSIGN with BACKUP, RESTORE, LABEL, JOIN, SUBST, or PRINT. FORMAT, DISKCOPY, and DISKCOMP ignore ASSIGN.

EXAMPLES

As already noted, ASSIGN is most commonly used in older programs that require you to place either your program disk in drive A or your data disk in drive B, or both. For instance, if you have copied all of your program and data files to a directory on drive C and then made that directory the current directory, you might enter

ASSIGN A=C B=C

This forces all program references to A and B to be handled from the current working directory on drive C.

You can apply the same principle if you have multiple disk drives and wish to use any other letters to represent diskette or hard-disk alternatives to the diskette drive identifiers originally specified by the application program.

The SUBST command is a more flexible alternative that allows you to work with multiple directories on a hard disk. For instance, if you are running a program called Oldstuff, you could copy all program diskette files to a directory called \OLDSTUFF and all of the former data disk files to a directory called \OLDSTUFF\DATA. You could then issue the following command:

SUBST A: C:\OLDSTUFF
SUBST B: C:\OLDSTUFF\DATA

SEE ALSO

SUBST

CHDIR (CD)

You can use CHDIR (or simply CD) to change directories as you move through the directory structure.

VERSION

Introduced in DOS 2.0

SYNTAX

C[H]D[IR] [*d:path*]

d:path represents the optional drive and path specifying the directory you wish to make the default directory.

TYPE

Internal.

USAGE

The CHDIR (or CD for short) command allows you to change the current working directory. DOS looks for executable files in the current working directory before searching the path; it looks for data files in the current working directory before searching the APPEND list. It is therefore often desirable to work in the current directory. The CD command is most often used to make a particular directory the current directory.

Executing CHDIR .. puts you in the immediate parent directory of the directory you are in. (The double-period symbol denotes the parent directory.) A *parent* directory is always one step up in the hierarchy; that is, it is the directory within which the current directory was created.

EXAMPLES

If you want to make the DATA subdirectory within the CAD directory your current working directory, enter

CD \CAD\DATA

To reset the current working directory to the root of your current drive, enter

**CD **

If you wish to make LOTUS\ACCOUNTS\JUDD the working directory, enter

CD \LOTUS\ACCOUNTS\JUDD

Entering CD with no parameters displays the current working directory for the default drive. To display the current working directory for any other drive, enter the drive name as a first parameter, as follows:

CD D:

CHKDSK

CHKDSK provides information about a disk, including size, available space and, in DOS 4, volume serial number.

VERSION

Introduced in DOS 1.0; enhanced first in DOS 2.0 and most recently in DOS 4.0

SYNTAX

[*d:path*]**CHKDSK** [*filespec*][**/F**][**/V**]

d:path	represents the drive and path where the command file is located if it is not in the current directory.
filespec	represents an optional drive and path, plus the file name and extension, of the file that is the object of the command. Wildcards are allowed.
/F	allows corrections to be made on the disk.
/V	lists all files and their paths.

TYPE

External.

USAGE

CHKDSK checks the formatted size and available space on a disk. It also indicates the amount of disk space consumed by system files, data files, and bad sectors, and indicates memory size and amount of memory available. The DOS 4 version also reports the volume serial number and information about the disk's allocation units (clusters). It is most often used simply to check the amount of available space on a disk. Sometimes, in situations where you are using memory-resident routines as well, CHKDSK is also used to assess the amount of available memory space. DOS 4's MEM command, however, provides this service and more.

EXAMPLES

The last two lines of the CHKDSK display indicate the total memory space and the amount of free memory. To check the status of your default disk drive, enter CHKDSK with no parameters:

CHKDSK

This command produces a report on your monitor like the following (assuming default drive C):

```
Volume DRIVE C      created 12-23-88   6:02pm
Volume Serial Number is 1838-3887

21213184 bytes total disk space
69632 bytes in 3 hidden files
59392 bytes in 20 directories
15036416 bytes in 846 user files
6047744 bytes available on disk

2048 bytes in each allocation unit
10358 total allocation units on disk
2987 available allocation units on disk

655360 total bytes memory
565504 bytes free
```

The serial numbers do not appear in DOS versions earlier than 4. Checking the status of another disk drive requires only the specification of the disk drive identifier:

CHKDSK B:

If errors are reported on a disk, you can do nothing about them unless you run the CHKDSK command using the /F switch; this instructs CHKDSK to adjust the file allocation table. Moreover, you must also answer Y to the question posed by the CHKDSK command about fixing the error. At this time, all lost allocation units (clusters) are recovered into a file named FILE*nnnn*.CHK. Since clusters appear on the disk in linked chains, each recovered chain is stored into a different file, with *nnnn* being adjusted to a different sequence of digits beginning with 0000.

DIR

The DIR command offers several ways for you to see what files are on a disk.

VERSION

Introduced in DOS 1.0; most recently enhanced in DOS 2.1

SYNTAX

DIR [*filespec*][**/P**][**/W**]

filespec — represents an optional drive and path, plus the file name and extension, of the file that is the object of the command.

/P — causes the computer to prompt you to continue listing directory entries if the listing is longer than one screen.

/W — causes the directory listing to be displayed in wide format (without listing the file size and the date and time of creation or modification), with entries listed horizontally as well as vertically.

All DIR parameters represented by *filespec* are completely independent of one another. They can be used in any combination, either alone or together, to limit the directory listing.

TYPE

Internal.

USAGE

DIR is one of the most commonly used DOS commands. Without this command, it would be extremely difficult, if not impossible, to operate a computer system of any size. It displays status information about files on a disk. Its various forms display the names of files on any disk, each file's size and date and time of creation or last modification, the number of free bytes on the drive you are referencing, and the total number of files on a drive that meet a specified criterion.

RESTRICTIONS

The DIR command does not list hidden files.

EXAMPLES

Suppose you had created a new directory (in anticipation of your upcoming switch to a new operating system) called OS2. Entering

DIR C:\OS2

displays the label (volume) of the disk in drive C and the name, size, and date and time of last modification of each file in the OS2 directory on drive C.

You can compact the display by eliminating the size, date, and time columns and displaying only the file names in five parallel columns. The /W switch manages the creation of this wide display:

DIR C: /W

This command displays the same file names for the current working directory of drive C as the preceding command. This time, however, only the file names are displayed, in five columns.

SEE ALSO

CHDIR
MKDIR
RMDIR
TREE

DOSSHELL

The DOSSHELL command enables DOS 4 users to initiate the graphic shell program from the standard DOS command line.

VERSION

Introduced in DOS 4.0

SYNTAX

[*d:path*]**DOSSHELL**

d:path represents the drive and path where the command file is located if it is not in the current directory.

TYPE

External.

USAGE

Entering the DOSSHELL command in DOS 4 will initiate the graphic shell program, a simple batch file created during the system installation process. This batch file switches the DOS command interface from a familiar command-line interface to the new graphic style used in DOS 4. This completely redesigned set of screens presents users with a series of on-screen windows containing directory, file, and DOS feature information. You can use either a keyboard or a mouse to access all functions, features, and files on a DOS 4 system. Enter this command at the startup command prompt if your system has been prepared to begin at the command level. You can also return to the graphic interface by entering DOSSHELL at a standard DOS command prompt. You can exit from the shell to the command prompt by pressing F3 or by selecting Exit from the Start Programs portion of the shell.

RESTRICTIONS

Do not use enter DOSSHELL if you are at a nested shell prompt (that is, a secondary command processor invoked from within the shell itself); this will consume unnecessary memory.

EXAMPLES

Suppose your DOSSHELL batch command file is located in your \DOS directory, which is not necessarily on your PATH or APPEND /X lists. Bring up the DOS 4 graphic shell by entering the following command:

```
\DOS\DOSSHELL
```

FORMAT

This command formats a disk for use with DOS.

VERSION

Introduced in DOS 1.0; enhanced first in DOS 2.0 and most recently in DOS 4.0

SYNTAX

[*d:path*]**FORMAT** *d1:*
[/S][/1][/4][/8][/V:*label***][/B][/N:***xx***][/T:***yy***][/F:***size***]**

d:path	represents the drive and path where the command file is located if it is not in the current directory.
d1:	represents the drive to be formatted.
/S	causes a system disk to be created. A hard disk should always be formatted as a system disk.
/1	formats only one side of a disk. This switch facilitates backward compatibility for a diskette that will be used on a DOS 1.X system. Version 1 of DOS was originally designed to handle single-sided disks only.
/4	causes a high-capacity drive to format a 360K, double-sided diskette.
/8	formats a diskette with 8 sectors instead of 9. Version 1 of DOS was originally designed to handle only 8 sectors per track.
/V:*label*	(in DOS 4 only) automatically assigns label as your disk label and creates a unique serial

number, which is written to the boot sector of the disk being formatted. The serial number is displayed for you at the end of the formatting process and can later be seen as part of the output of other DOS commands, such as CHKDSK. Earlier versions of DOS had only a /V switch, which requested that FORMAT prompt you for the entry of a volume label; if /V were not included, the disk was formatted without a label at all. Since DOS 4 requires volume labels and serial number identification, you will be prompted for a label if you neglect to specify one with this switch.

/B	formats a diskette with 8 sectors and leaves room for the hidden system files, but it does not transfer the system to the disk, thus allowing the use of the SYS command with any DOS version, especially the earlier versions, which expect only 8 sectors per track.
/N:*xx*	formats a disk with *xx* sectors per track. This parameter is required if you use multiple machines and prepare diskettes on one for use on another.
/T:*yy*	formats a disk with *yy* tracks. This parameter is required if you use multiple machines and prepare diskettes on one for use on another.
/F:*size*	(in DOS 4 only) offers users an easy way of formatting diskettes to sizes that are smaller than the nominal capacity of the drive they are being formatted in.

TYPE

External.

USAGE

FORMAT is used regularly with all new diskettes fresh from the box. It is also used to reformat older, used diskettes; in addition to clearing the disk of all old data, using FORMAT with old disks helps protect you and your disks from the deleterious effects of possible bad sectors.

Hard disks must also be formatted. The command is the same as for diskettes, although many FORMAT options are not relevant to hard disks. Because formatting erases any information already on the disk, this step is generally taken only once, after FDISK has been used to create a primary DOS partition on a new disk. (Your computer dealer may have done this when you bought the machine.) Any extended DOS partitions you create with FDISK (see Appendix D) must also be formatted before you can use them.

RESTRICTIONS

FORMAT ignores assignments made with ASSIGN. You cannot use the /V switch to format a diskette for DOS 1.1. You must use the /V switch in DOS 4 to assign a label to a disk; otherwise, you will be prompted to enter one. A 360KB diskette formatted in a high-capacity drive cannot be read reliably in single- or double-density drives. If you need a formatted 360KB diskette in another machine, format it in that other machine; it then can be reliably written on by a high-capacity drive.

EXAMPLES

As an extra protection, FORMAT requires you to enter the current volume label when you try to format a hard disk. If your hard disk does not have a volume label, press ↵ to begin the formatting. DOS will not format a disk if the volume label you enter does not match the label it finds on the disk. For instance, if you enter the command FORMAT D: for a hard disk and then enter a volume identifier different from the one DOS actually finds on the disk, DOS displays this message:

```
Invalid Volume ID
Format Failure.
```

If the volume labels match, DOS gives you a last chance to back out of this potentially disastrous procedure, in which all data on your disk will be lost:

```
WARNING!
ALL DATA ON THE FIXED DISK DRIVE D: WILL BE LOST!
PROCEED WITH FORMAT (Y/N)?
```

A simple and common use of the FORMAT command is to format a diskette in drive A to use as much space as the drive allows. To do this, enter

FORMAT A:

In DOS 3.31 and earlier, you must enter the following command to create a system diskette with a volume label:

FORMAT A: /S /V

In this example, DOS formats the disk, copies the operating system files onto it, and prompts you to enter a volume label. This volume label identifies your disk; you should write a volume label each time you format a new disk. The label can contain up to 11 characters of any kind, including spaces.

In DOS 4, you can use the /V:*label* switch to specify the volume label when you enter the FORMAT command:

FORMAT A: /S /V:INVENTORY

In this example, DOS formats the disk, copies the operating system files onto it, labels the disk with the character string INVENTORY, then creates and writes a unique serial number into the boot sector of the disk.

Also in DOS 4, it becomes very simple to format differently sized disk media. For instance, to format a 720K 3½-inch diskette in a 1.44M 3½-inch drive requires only the addition of the /F:720 switch. To give the presumed data disk the label ACCOUNTING at the same time, you would enter

FORMAT A: /F:720 /V:ACCOUNTING

JOIN

JOIN permits an entirely separate disk drive and all its contents to be perceived and referenced as if they were a branch of the directory structure on a second drive.

VERSION

Introduced in DOS 3.1

SYNTAX

(1) [*d:path*]**JOIN**
(2) [*d:path*]**JOIN** *object source*
(3) [*d:path*]**JOIN** *object* **/D**

d:path	represents the drive and path where the command file is located if it is not in the current directory.
object	represents the drive to which a directory will be attached or released.
source	represents the drive and path of the directory to be joined.
/D	nullifies a previously defined JOIN and restores normalcy

TYPE

External.

USAGE

JOIN is used primarily to transmit data to or from a file on a diskette when a program tries to transfer data to or from a directory. It is used to fool older programs into using hierarchical disk structures when they were designed to understand only individual disk drives (usually drives A and B).

RESTRICTIONS

You can use JOIN only on multidisk systems. You cannot use this command to join a drive created with SUBST.

EXAMPLES

The JOIN command is used primarily in two ways. If a program is sending information to a fixed subdirectory on drive C, such as C:\CAD\DATA, and you wish to send this information directly to a diskette in drive A, enter

JOIN A: C:\CAD\DATA

On the other hand, if you want the output of a program designed to send data to the root directory of drive B sent to the current working directory of drive C, and you have changed the working directory (with CD) to that desired subdirectory on drive C before running the program, enter

JOIN C: B:

to join drive C to the root directory of drive B.

To restore normalcy and nullify a previously defined JOIN, use the /D switch. For example, to disconnect drive C from the root directory of drive B, enter

JOIN C: /D

LABEL

LABEL allows you to label your disk volumes electronically. These disk names will appear each time you call up a directory.

VERSION

Introduced in DOS 3.0

SYNTAX

[*d:path*]**LABEL** [*d1*:][*string*]

d:path represents the drive and path where the command file is located if it is not listed in the current directory.

d1: represents the drive containing the disk whose label is to be changed or displayed.

string when specified, becomes the label of the disk in *d1*.

TYPE

External.

USAGE

If you know the contents of a particular disk and want to give that disk a new electronic label, you can do so most quickly with the LABEL command. LABEL is most often used to assign volume identifiers to older disks that were not labeled during the formatting process. Note that disks formatted with the FORMAT program available in DOS version 1 cannot accept volume labels, even those assigned with the LABEL command.

RESTRICTIONS

You cannot use LABEL with drives that have been substituted or joined.

You cannot use the following characters in a volume label: * ? / \ | . , ; : + = < > [ ] ( ) @ ^.

EXAMPLES

Assume that you want to label the disk in drive B with the name BUDGETS. Enter

LABEL B: BUDGETS

If you are not sure what is currently on a disk, you can use the LABEL command to display the current volume label. For example, entering

LABEL B:

produces the following results:

```
Volume in drive B is BUDGETS
   Type a volume label of up to 11 characters or
Press Enter for no volume label update: _
```

SEE ALSO

FORMAT

MKDIR (MD)

The MKDIR command (or MD for short) creates a new directory, either in the current working directory or at the specified path location in an existing tree.

VERSION

Introduced in DOS 2.0

SYNTAX

M[K]D[IR] [*d:path*]

d:path represents the optional drive and path specifying the directory you wish to create.

TYPE

Internal.

USAGE

The MKDIR command enables you to make new directories, which helps you organize files on any disk. As with all other file references, you can specify a file name without entering the complete path, and DOS will assume that the reference is to the current working directory.

The new directory initially will be empty of files, but it is usable immediately.

EXAMPLES

No matter what directory you are using, you can also create a new subdirectory, called DATA, within it by entering

MD DATA

Assuming that your current working directory is \SYMPHONY, you have effectively created a data directory with the full path name of \SYMPHONY\DATA.

You do not need to place the new subdirectory in the current directory. For example, your working directory can be located in drive A, and you can use the MD command to create a new INFO subdirectory within the SCHOOL directory, located in drive D:

MD D:\SCHOOL\INFO

SEE ALSO

RMDIR (RD)

PATH

The PATH Command sets or resets the sequence of directories (that is, the path) to be searched for executable files.

VERSION

Introduced in DOS 2.0

SYNTAX

PATH [*d1:path1*][;*d2:path2*...]

[*d1:path1*]	represents the first drive and directory searched.
[*d2:path2...*]	represents the second drive and directory searched, and so on.

TYPE

Internal.

USAGE

PATH is a command you are likely to use frequently. It sets or resets the sequence of directories to be searched for executable files, whether they be .COM, .EXE, or .BAT files. In the typical DOS application setup, you select a default directory for data files and then specify a PATH list to locate the executable file to run.

Use PATH when you need to access a program in a directory other than the current one. The PATH command gives DOS a list of drives and directories to search in a specified order until it finds the requested program file. Be careful when specifying a search sequence: If there are two different files with the same name in different directories along the path, DOS will use the first one it encounters.

RESTRICTIONS

PATH will not work with data, overlay, or other nonexecutable files (see APPEND).

EXAMPLES

The following entry instructs DOS to search the root directory, then the 123 directory, and finally the UTILITY directory to locate any external commands or programs not in the current working directory:

PATH \;\123;\UTILITY

SEE ALSO

APPEND

RMDIR (RD)

After deleting all files and subdirectories in a directory, use the RMDIR command to delete the directory.

VERSION

Introduced in DOS 2.0

SYNTAX

R[M]D[IR] [*d:path*]

d:path	represents the drive and path of the directory to be removed.

TYPE

Internal.

USAGE

You will probably use RMDIR only infrequently. Typically, you use this command only to clean up a messy hard-disk directory structure. After you erase all files in an individual directory, that directory may no longer be needed and so can be removed from the hierarchy. Removing unnecessary directories makes the remaining structure clearer and easier to understand. Using the familiar tree analogy, removing directories is comparable to pruning dead branches.

RESTRICTIONS

You cannot remove a directory until all files and subdirectories within it have been deleted or removed by a separate operation.

EXAMPLES

To remove an empty directory, such as OLDSTUFF in the DBMS directory, enter

RD \DBMS\OLDSTUFF

If OLDSTUFF isn't empty, use DIR to display existing file names or to determine which subdirectories still exist within it. You can then use the ERASE command to delete the files in those directories or the RD command to remove an existing subdirectory.

If your current working directory is already DBMS, you need only indicate OLDSTUFF as the object of RD:

RD OLDSTUFF

SUBST

SUBST enables you to access files using either their complete path name or a shorthand notation.

VERSION

Introduced in DOS 3.1

SYNTAX

(1) [*d:path*]**SUBST**
(2) [*d:path*]**SUBST** *newdrive source*
(3) [*d:path*]**SUBST** *object* **/D**

d:path	represents the drive and path where the command file is located if it is not in the current directory.
newdrive	represents the drive to be created to correspond to the *source* directory.
source	represents the directory to be made into drive *newdrive*.
object	represents the pseudodrive identifier used as *newdrive* and now to be discarded.
/D	nullifies any previous SUBST command.

TYPE

External.

USAGE

The SUBST command is often used to cut down on the typing needed to refer to file names located within a complex directory structure. It is easier to type a single letter and a colon than a complete path name.

You can substitute a single letter identifier—that is, a pseudo disk-drive letter—for a complete directory path name leading to a particular file.

EXAMPLES

The following example creates a virtual drive, G, as a substitute for D:\PROGRAMS\WORDPROC\WORDPERF, the complete path name:

```
SUBST G: D:\PROGRAMS\WORDPROC\WORDPERF
```

All succeeding references to files in the WORDPERF subdirectory can now use either the full path name or the simpler G: designation.

You can also use this technique to fool older programs that understand only disk drives without a directory structure. For example, suppose you have a geometric analysis program called GEOMETRY.EXE. This program requires its own system and support files to be on drive A and all of its data files to exist or be created on drive B. You can create subdirectories within your disk hierarchy called \GEOMETRY and \GEOMETRY\DATA and then use SUBST to trick your original programs into accessing program files from the GEOMETRY directory and data files from the DATA directory:

```
SUBST A: \GEOMETRY
SUBST B: \GEOMETRY\DATA
```

TREE

TREE displays a list of all of your directories and subdirectories and the files they contain.

VERSION

Introduced in DOS 2.0; most recently enhanced in DOS 4.0

SYNTAX

[*d:path*]TREE [*d2*:][/F]

d:path	represents the drive and path where the command file is located if the file is not in the current directory.
d2	represents the drive identifier of another drive you want TREE to affect.
/F	displays all paths and file names in the directories.
/A	uses an alternate graphic character set, or code page, for drawing the tree. Available only in DOS 4.

TYPE

External.

USAGE

The primary role of the TREE command is to display the hierarchy of directories and subdirectories for a particular disk drive. Such a display is especially useful for examining the directory structure to determine where pruning might improve efficiency. The list shown is textual in DOS versions 3.31 and earlier; it is a graphic representation in DOS 4. The volume label (and volume serial number in DOS 4) are also displayed as part of this output.

EXAMPLES

To display each directory on the current drive, and each subdirectory within each directory, simply enter

TREE

Use the /F switch with this command to produce a listing of all files, listed by directory, for your disk drive. The output containing the file listing typically appears on your video monitor. However, using an advanced DOS feature called redirection allows you to specify where you want the output listing to go. The output redirection operator is a chevron symbol, >, and can be added to the end of any DOS command. You can redirect a command's output to a printer (> PRN) or to any specifically named disk file. Combining this TREE command with redirection allows you to produce a complete log of all files on a disk, store the log in a new file, and then later print this log file:

TREE D: /F > files.log

VOL

The VOL command shows the volume label of a disk in a specified drive.

VERSION

Introduced in DOS 2.0; enhanced in DOS 4

SYNTAX

VOL *[d:]*

d	is a specified drive, if different from the default drive.

TYPE

Resident.

USAGE

Entering the VOL command alone causes DOS to display the label of the current working disk drive. It's quick, if that's all the information you need. Since the DIR command always displays the disk's volume ID, this command is not invoked very often.

In DOS 4, the VOL display includes the volume serial number.

EXAMPLES

On a system using DOS 3.31 or earlier, entering

VOL

is likely to produce this result:

```
Volume in drive C is drive ID
```

CHAPTER 2

File-Management Commands

All computer systems depend on two principal types of files: program and data files. A *program* file is one that can be executed or run; a *data* file is one containing information that can be acted on in some way to produce meaningful results. Managing your system's files is critical to your success with DOS. This chapter presents the most important file management commands used in DOS to control, influence, and affect the data within your disk's files, regardless of the type of file itself.

ATTRIB

The ATTRIB command displays or changes the read/write and archive attributes of a file.

VERSION

Introduced in DOS 3.0; enhanced in DOS 3.3

SYNTAX

[*d:path*]**ATTRIB [+R | −R][+A | −A]**[*filespec*]**[/S]**

d:path	represents the drive and path where the command file is located if it is not in the current directory.
+R	makes *filespec* a read-only file.
−R	makes *filespec* read/write operations possible.
+A	sets the archive bit of *filespec*.
−A	resets the archive bit of *filespec*.
filespec	represents an optional drive and path, plus the file name and extension, of the file that is the object of the command. Wildcards are allowed.
/S	applies the command to all files in the directory and its subdirectories.

TYPE

External.

USAGE

When used with parameters, ATTRIB changes specified attributes of a file. When used without parameters, ATTRIB simply displays the attributes.

The ATTRIB command is most commonly used to set one or more files to read-only status. This prevents a file from being accidentally or purposely deleted and also inhibits any editing or modification of the file. While +R makes a specified file read-only, adding the /S switch extends the protection to all files located in a specified directory and its subdirectories with a single command.

ATTRIB is also used in network applications. It enforces read-only status of files intended to be shared by multiple users across the network.

EXAMPLES

To set read-only status for the BUDGET.WK1 file, you enter

ATTRIB +R BUDGET.WK1

Since wildcards are allowed, you can just as easily turn on read-only status for all personnel data files in the PERSONEL directory, including .TXT, .WK1, and .DBF, files:

ATTRIB +R PERSONEL.*

The /S switch adjusts the attributes of all files in the entire directory tree starting with the specified directory. For example, you can remove the read-only status of all files on a disk with the following command:

ATTRIB -R C:\ /S

The A (archive) attribute controls the archival status of a file. Several DOS commands, including BACKUP, RESTORE, XCOPY, COPY, REPLACE, and PRINT, use this archive attribute to decide whether to include a file during their operation. You can influence their operation by presetting the +A or -A status of a file. These other commands have switches, such as /M or /A, which are influenced directly by the setting of the file's archive attribute, as set here by the ATTRIB command.

SEE ALSO

BACKUP
RESTORE
XCOPY

BACKUP

BACKUP selectively makes backup copies of specified files.

VERSION

Introduced in DOS 2.0; enhanced first in DOS 3.3 and most recently in DOS 4.0

SYNTAX

[*location*]**BACKUP** *source dest switches*

location	represents the drive and path where the command file is located if it is not in the current directory.	
source	represents the drive, path, and optional file specification to be backed up.	
dest	represents the drive on which the backup will be made.	
switches	represents any one or combination of the following:	
	/S	backs up all subdirectories within the directory specified in source.
	/M	backs up only those files that have been changed since the last backup.
	/A	adds the files that will be backed up to those already on dest, thus not destroying existing files on dest.

/D:*mm-dd-yy*	backs up files changed on or after the date specified (the format depends on the country selected).
/T:*hh-mm-ss*	backs up files changed at or after the time specified (the format depends on the country selected).
/F	executes the program FORMAT.COM (which should be available) on any *dest* disk not already formatted.
/L[:*filespec*]	creates a log file with the given file name in the specified directory on a disk (the default name is BACKUP.LOG in the root directory of *source*).

TYPE

External.

USAGE

BACKUP is preferred over XCOPY for backing up your hard disk for several reasons. The most important reason is that XCOPY can back up only onto one diskette. If a file takes up more space than is available on a diskette, as does a 5MB database file, for example, you cannot use any DOS command other than BACKUP to back it up. BACKUP automatically breaks up large files and saves them on multiple diskettes (prompting you to insert a new diskette when necessary).

BACKUP also saves long lists of files that together need more than one diskette for storage. Furthermore, for DOS 4 users, BACKUP automatically formats the target diskette if you neglected to format it previously.

Make sure that you have the VERIFY command ON for making backups. It's worth the extra time for the peace of mind that the backup copies are 100% accurate.

RESTRICTIONS

You cannot back up files that you are sharing but do not have access to. Do not use BACKUP with JOIN, SUBST, APPEND, or ASSIGN in effect. Unless you use the /A parameter, BACKUP will erase all the files on the destination disk. The target disk will be formatted according to the capacity of the drive. Mismatches in capacity or formatting are not allowed.

Also, since the DOS 4 version of BACKUP can automatically format a diskette, the DOS FORMAT command must be available in the current directory or located on the DOS directory PATH list.

EXAMPLES

A common and simple backup technique is writing copies of all files on a hard disk to a set of backup diskettes:

BACKUP C:\ B: /S

In this example command, the source directory on drive C is the root (\), the destination drive is drive B, and the /S switch ensures that all subordinate directories on drive C are copied during the backup operation.

Another common backup operation is backing up all files within a single hard disk directory to a set of floppy disks. Entering

BACKUP C:\WP*.WSD B:

backs up word processing files with extension .WSD from the WP directory. All files are written to successive diskettes on drive B.

SEE ALSO

COPY
XCOPY

COMP

COMP compares two or more files to see if they are the same.

VERSION

Introduced in DOS 1.0; revised in DOS 2.0.

SYNTAX

[*d:path*]**COMP** [*filespec1*] [*filespec2*]

d:path	represents the drive and path where the command file is located if it is not in the current directory.
filespec1	represents the optional drive and path, plus the file names and extensions, of the first set of files to be compared. Wildcards are allowed.
filespec2	represents the optional drive and path, plus the file names and extensions, of the second set of files to be compared. Wildcards are allowed.

TYPE

External.

USAGE

The COMP command is used to compare the contents of two or more files. A common application is to compare whether two files located in separate directories are identical. COMP is also used to verify whether two programs on different disks with different dates are simply replicas of one another, acquired or created at different times.

EXAMPLES

The following command line verifies whether the version of BUDGET.TXT in the current working directory is identical to the file of the same name located in the BUDGET directory:

COMP C:\LOTUS\BUDGET\BUDGET.TXT BUDGET.TXT

You can also use wildcards to compare multiple files with different extensions. In the following example, all word processing files with a .WP extension are compared with all word processing files with a .WPB extension to determine which files are identical to their backup versions (had no changes made in the most recent edit):

COMP \WP*.WP \WP*.WPB

This command is most useful for verifying that the contents of two files are the same, but it is less useful to most users for determining exactly what the differences are. This is because the results of COMP are presented using hexadecimal notation, not the original source code. COMP returns values for the bytes that are different and for the offset into the files. For nonprogrammers, this information is of little or no use.

COPY

The COPY command has three distinct uses. You can use it to duplicate files, to access devices, or to concatenate files.

VERSION

Introduced in DOS 1.0; enhanced in DOS 1.1

SYNTAX

1. Use this format to duplicate files:

   COPY [**/A**][**/B**]*sourcefile* [[**/A**][**/B**][*destfile*][**/A**][**/B**][**/V**]]

2. Use this format to access devices:

   COPY [**/A**][**/B**]*source* [**/A**][**/B**][*dest*][**/A**][**/B**][**/V**]

3. Use this format to concatenate files:

   COPY
   [**/A**][**/B**]*sourcefile1* + *sourcefile2*[**/A**][**/B**] + ...[*concatfile*][**/A**][**/B**][**/V**]

/A is used with *sourcefile*, *source*, or *sourcefile-1+sourcefile2* to read data up to but not including the first Ctrl-Z (end-of-file) character; the file is treated as an ASCII file. This is the default setting for concatenation (format 3). The /A switch is used with *destfile*, *dest*, or *concatfile* to write a Ctrl-Z character at the end of the file.

/B is the default setting for file duplication (format 1). It is used with *sourcefile*, *source*, or

	sourcefile1 + *sourcefile2* to copy a number of bytes equal to the number of bytes given as the length in the directory for the file. The /B switch is used with *destfile*, *dest*, or *concatfile* to make sure that no Ctrl-Z character is written at the end of the file.
/V	causes DOS to check whether all files were copied successfully. It is used only with transfers to disk files.
sourcefile	represents the drive, path, file name, and extension of the file to be copied.
destfile	represents the drive, path, file name, and extension of the file to which *sourcefile* will be copied.
source and *dest*	can be either device or file specifications, although DOS allows only ASCII files to be read from a device.
sourcefile1 and *sourcefile2*	represent files to be added together (*sourcefile2* is added to the end of *sourcefile1*, and so on).
ConcatFile	represents the file that contains the concatenation of the source files.

These switches affect the file immediately preceding the place where the switch is used, as well as all files following it, until the next time the switch is used.

TYPE

Internal.

USAGE

Duplicating files with COPY, using the first format of this command, allows you versatility in moving files around the disk system. You can copy the contents of entire directories and then move them to another disk. Without COPY, you could not transfer newly purchased programs from diskettes to your hard disk or copy files to a diskette for another system.

The second format of COPY is especially useful for printing multiple files at once, which cannot be done with the TYPE command.

The third format of the COPY command allows files to be concatenated; that is, one ASCII-type files can be added to the end of another to form one large file.

Note that copies of read-only files created with COPY will not be read-only files. (You can use the ATTRIB command to make the copied file read only.) Note also that if you do not specify a destination file in the third format of the COPY command, all source files will be appended to the end of the first source file.

EXAMPLES

To copy the file SK.COM from a diskette in drive A to a drive C directory containing utility software, enter the following command:

```
COPY A:SK.COM C:\UTILITY
```

All copies placed in the UTILITY directory have the same name as the original file on the diskette in drive A.

Copying all files from a new application program to a newly created directory on a hard disk is easy with the COPY command. The following sequence makes the DBMS directory the current default directory on drive C and then copies all files from the drive A diskette into that directory:

```
CD \DBMS
COPY A:*.*
```

You can also make a backup directory to house backup copies of all spreadsheet files, for example. The following command sequence creates a backup directory and then transfers all WK1 files into that directory, giving them new extensions (WKB) in the process. The base names of the files remain the same.

```
MD \LOTUS\BACKUPS
CD \LOTUS\DATA
COPY *.WK1 \LOTUS\BACKUPS\*.WKB
```

You can also use COPY to consolidate a group of text files, so that you can more easily edit small files with a word processor, possibly to produce a consolidated report. The following example combines three separate text files into one.

COPY STUDY.TXT + RESULTS.TXT + ANALYSIS.TXT SUMMARY.RPT

The separate text files—STUDY, REPORT, and ANALYSIS—are merged into a new file called SUMMARY.RPT. The new report file is created on the default drive with the current date and time. Be sure to specify a destination file, such as SUMMARY.RPT. If you do not, DOS combines the files and places them in the first specified file of the collection. (You may sometimes want the files placed in the first specified file to avoid specifying a separate destination file.)

You can also use wildcards to combine several files. For example, you can combine all files with the .TXT extension into one complete report with the following command:

COPY *.TXT TOTAL.RPT

SEE ALSO

BACKUP
XCOPY

DEL

This command removes files from the directory.

VERSION

Introduced in DOS 1.1; most recently enhanced in DOS 4.0

SYNTAX

DEL ***filespec*** **/P**

filespec represents an optional drive and path, plus the file name and extension, of each file to be deleted. Wildcards are allowed. You can specify only a drive and path, omitting any filename(s), in which case all files in the specified directory are deleted.

/P prompts you to enter Y or N for each filename selected for deletion.

TYPE

Internal.

USAGE

The DEL command is most often used to erase an individual file by specifying its name to free up space on a disk. The files are still physically present on the disk and can be retrieved by using certain non-DOS disk utilities (such as Norton Utilities, discussed in Chapter 4), but it is not accessible using the directory structure. The other most common use for this command, using wildcards, removes all files from a diskette or from a subdirectory of a hard disk.

An alternate command, ERASE, performs exactly the same function as DEL. Many users prefer the ERASE command because its letters are more distinct from the three-letter command DIR.

When you issue the command DEL *.*, which deletes all files in the current directory, DOS displays the warning "Are you sure (Y/N)?" to verify that you really wish to take such a drastic action. Issuing the DEL command with a subdirectory as the filespec parameter deletes all files in that subdirectory, but not the subdirectory itself. You must use the RD command to remove an empty subdirectory.

RESTRICTIONS

You cannot use DEL to delete read-only files or any subdirectory that still contains files.

EXAMPLES

You can delete an individual file or use wildcards to delete multiple files at the same time. The following example deletes the file 1987.WK1:

DEL 1987.WK1

You can use a wildcard to delete all backup files in any directory. For example, the following command deletes all backup files from the DBMS directory:

DEL \DBMS*.BAK

You can erase the complete contents of any particular directory by specifying the directory name itself as a parameter of this command. For example, to remove all files from the \CAD\DATA directory, enter

DEL \CAD\DATA /P

Because of the /P switch, each filename in the \CAD\DATA directory will be successively displayed for you with the repeated verification prompt:

Filename, DELETE (Y/N)?

SEE ALSO

RD

ERASE

The ERASE command is identical to the DEL command. See DEL in this chapter for syntax and examples.

FASTOPEN

FASTOPEN speeds up disk access by maintaining a memory-resident table of the most recently used file and directory names. It also has a disk-caching feature discussed in EXAMPLES.

VERSION

Introduced in DOS 3.3; enhanced in DOS 4.0

SYNTAX

[*d:path*]**FASTOPEN** *drive*:[= *size*,*buf*][*drive*:[= *size*,*buf*][...]]

d:path represents the drive and path where the command file is located if it is not in the current directory.

drive represents the drive to which FASTOPEN will be attached.

size represents the number of file or directory entries that FASTOPEN will remember.

buf represents the number of contiguous memory buffers reserved in memory for storing actual file data from most recently used files.

/X directs FASTOPEN to use expanded memory for its buffer space.

TYPE

External.

USAGE

FASTOPEN is normally used to ensure more rapid disk access to the most frequently referenced disk sectors of either directory or file information. These include the actual files commonly accessed as well as the sectors containing the directory entries for those files. FASTOPEN also can maintain a memory cache of actual file data from the most recently opened files. These two features can be set up independently for multiple disk drives with one FASTOPEN statement.

Ideally, you should set the value for FASTOPEN on each referenced drive equal to the minimum number of frequently referenced file names plus the number of directory entries in the full path names leading to those files.

RESTRICTIONS

FASTOPEN will not work with JOIN, SUBST, or ASSIGN in effect on the designated drive. It also will not work with network drives. Using the /X switch for expanded memory requires that you install the special device drivers XMAEM.SYS and XMA2EMS-.SYS in your CONFIG.SYS file. The sum of all size parameters cannot exceed 999, and similarly, the sum of all *buf* parameters cannot exceed 999.

EXAMPLES

The FASTOPEN command is easy to use. Simply typing

FASTOPEN C: = 100

enables the computer to remember the last 100 directories and files accessed on drive C and thus to be able to go right to them on the disk. For example, suppose that size was specified as 5 rather than 100, and the list contained the information

DIR1 FILE1 DIR2 FILE2 FILE3

If you then accessed another FILE4 in directory DIR3, the list would look like this:

```
FILE4 DIR3 DIR1 FILE1 DIR2
```

FILE2 and FILE3 were the least-recent entries in the list, so they were dropped off the end to accommodate the two new entries.

You can use FASTOPEN only once per drive (per session). It reserves 35 bytes per entry. Thus, a size of 100 would consume about 3.5K (3,500) bytes of memory.

Specify size as a value at least as great as the highest number of levels in the directory structure, so DOS can quickly locate any directory specification.

In addition to the size parameter, you can include a value for the second parameter, buf. This sets up what is commonly called a "disk cache," consisting of a number of contiguous memory-resident buffers. Whereas the file buffers enable DOS to quickly locate the proper disk directory or file quickly, the buf buffers actually enable DOS to read the most recently accessed file data from these stored memory locations rather than going back to the disk. For example

```
FASTOPEN D: = 50,20
```

sets DOS up to hold up to 50 directory/file name entries in memory. It also stores memory copies of the 20 most recent buffers worth of data that are read from disk files.

Both rapid directory/filename access and file caching are independently set up with the following FASTOPEN statement:

```
FASTOPEN C: = 100   D: = 50,20   E: = ,65
```

This sets up directory/filename entry access on drives C and D but sets up file data caching only on drive D and E. The sole comma before the second parameter (65) in the E: specification makes it clear to FASTOPEN that 65 is the second entry and that there is no first size entry at all. In this way, using a comma and a second parameter value establishes a disk cache for file data but does not enable any system recall for directory/file names.

MORE

The MORE command pauses the display after each screenful of data.

VERSION

Introduced in DOS 2.0

SYNTAX

[*d:path*]**MORE**

d:path represents the drive and path where the command file is located if it is not in the current directory.

TYPE

External.

USAGE

The MORE command is typically used as a filter to read information from standard input, from a pipe, or from a redirected file. It always displays a screenful of information at a time and usually is used to enable the easy perusal of long text files by displaying only one screen of information at a time.

This command is similar to the DIR/P command, which pauses the directory listing after each screenful of data and asks you to press a key to continue. MORE is a filter—that is, data is sent to it, and MORE processes the data and sends it out in a new format. In this case, the filter simply prints the data a screenful at a time and prints "– MORE –" at the bottom of the screen until you press a key.

EXAMPLES

You can look at a prepared text report by using the MORE command with redirection techniques:

MORE < ANALYSIS.RPT

The < symbol is a redirection operator that allows you to specify the source of a command's input. Normally, this input comes from you at the keyboard. However, as you see here, you can prepare a disk file, which can be used as rapid input to a DOS command. In this example, the entire ANALYSIS.RPT file is used as input to the MORE command which displays the contents of the file, one full screen at a time.

With the SORT command, you can use MORE as a filter to provide a sorted display of the contents of any text file, one screenful at a time:

SORT ACCOUNTS.TXT | MORE

In this example, the ACCOUNTS.TXT file is first input to the SORT command. Following this, the special piping symbol (|) indicates that the sorted output is not to be sent directly to the screen, as would normally be the case. Instead, it is to be sent as input to the MORE command. MORE displays its input data (in this case, the sorted ACCOUNTS.TXT information) on your video monitor, one screenful at a time.

SEE ALSO

SORT

PRINT

As a file-management command, PRINT is used to invoke, modify, and add files to an internal, software-based queue, so that you can automatically output multiple files in order.

VERSION

Introduced in DOS 2.0

SYNTAX

[*location*]**PRINT** [*parameters*][*switches*][*dest1, ...*]

location — represents the drive and path where the command file is located if it is not in the current directory.

parameters — are optional redefinitions of the queue characteristics. You can enter these only the first time you set up a new print queue. They can be any of the following:

- /D: *device* — specifies the output device. The default setting is PRN (or LPT1). If you specify /D, it must be the first parameter specified.
- /B: *buffsize* — specifies the size of PRINT's output buffer in bytes. The default value is 512 bytes.
- /U: *busyticks* — specifies how much time, measured in ticks, the

PRINT command waits each cycle for a busy signal. The default setting is 1 tick.

/M: *maxticks* — specifies how much time, measured in ticks, the spooler has available for sending data to the printer before switching processing control to another job. The default setting is 2.

/S: *timeslice* — specifies how many time slices the computer allocates to the PRINT spooler every cycle. This value must be between 1 and 255, with 8 the default.

/Q: *queuesize* — specifies the maximum number of entries in the queue. This value may range from 1 to 32; the default value is 10.

switches — are optional settings that can be any of the following:

/C — cancels all previous and following entries on the command line.

/T — terminates the queue. All files queued are canceled from the queue.

/P — adds previous and all following entries on the command line to the queue.

dest1, ... — represents an optional list of files with their respective paths, names, and extensions to be queued for printing.

TYPE

External.

USAGE

The PRINT command contains a built-in capability called *spooling*, for *s*imultaneous *p*eripheral *o*perations *o*n-*l*ine. The spooling logic keeps track of all files awaiting printing. Even though other system operations may be occurring, spooling ensures that printing operations are effectively interleaved with other activity. It works by *slicing* up available processor time and assigning it to the jobs to be performed.

The amount of time the spooler needs to perform operations is defined in *clock ticks*. Just as musicians use a metronome to tick off time and to adjust their playing, a computer uses an internal clock, which ticks every fraction of a second (usually nanoseconds or milliseconds).

A *time slice* is a very short amount of time, usually equal to a user-specified number of clock ticks. The computer allocates part of its cycle to one task and part to another task. It does this by allocating a certain number of time slices to each task, as shown in Figure 2.1. Scheduling jobs by the larger time slice, rather than the smaller clock tick, reduces the administrative overhead. DOS juggles its available processing time between the primary, or foreground, application program and the secondary, or background, print-spooling job.

This diagram shows a unit of time divided into 255 slices—hence, *time slices*. Each slice represents the time the CPU spends on a certain task. Operating systems have either scheduling algorithms, or built-in logic that determines how many time slices are allocated to one task before the system moves on to another task. If the CPU allocates 200 time slices every cycle to input from the keyboard, there will be much idle time during which no effective processing is accomplished; during much of this time, the computer will simply wait for a user to enter new keyboard information or commands.

Thus, to give the illusion that it executes printing at the same time it executes another task, the computer spends one or more time slices on your printing job, and one or more time slices on your other keyboard requests. This explains why DOS seems to slow down slightly when

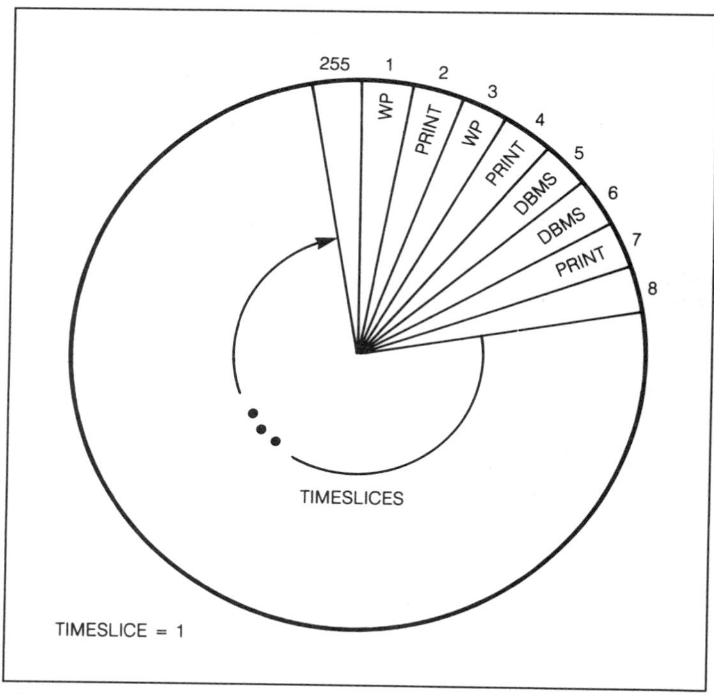

Figure 2.1: Time slicing

printing occurs concurrently with other work. DOS is spending some of its total processing time and power elsewhere (on the printing) and devotes less attention to you during each total cycle.

The PRINT command follows certain rules, all specified by its parameters. Figure 2.2 illustrates the flow of operations dictated by these rules. Assuming that some foreground task, such as word processing (WP), is processing, control will pass from WP to PRINT after a length of time (less than or equal to *timeslice*). When DOS passes control from a foreground application, such as WP, to the background PRINT task, PRINT first checks for printer availability. It waits up to the number of clock ticks specified in the *busyticks* parameter (phase A). (The higher value you assign to *busyticks*, the slower the system will run, since the system must wait for a busy printer. You should increase the value of *busyticks* only if you purposely want to maximize printer throughput, since increasing its value lends increased importance to printer output versus CPU processing.) If the printer becomes available in that time, PRINT begins to transmit data to the printer for printing. It does this for a number of clock ticks equal to *maxticks* (phase B).

For example, if you leave all default settings in effect, a sample operation would be as follows: DOS allows the CPU to work on your word processor for 8 time slices; then it's the spooler's turn. If you've just invoked PRINT, DOS first checks to make sure the printer is connected and uses two ticks of time to spool data. When the spooler's time is used up, DOS switches the CPU to another task, perhaps the word processor again. At some future time, the spooler again regains processing control. When DOS returns to the printer, DOS checks whether the printer is still printing the previously transmitted data. If printing has finished, the entire cycle is repeated. If the previously requested printing is still executing, the computer keeps testing the printer, and if it hasn't completed the printing task within *busytick* ticks, PRINT forfeits its current time allocation, and DOS skips to the next task, returning to the printer later.

If the *maxticks* number is large, the spooler sends much data, but also requires much computer time. If it is small, not much data can be sent, but the overall computer system runs faster. However, if the number is too small, your printer may slow down. Figure 2.3 shows

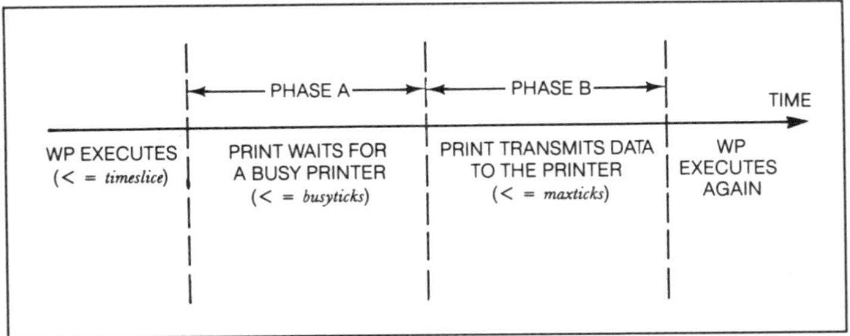

Figure 2.2: Flow of PRINT operations

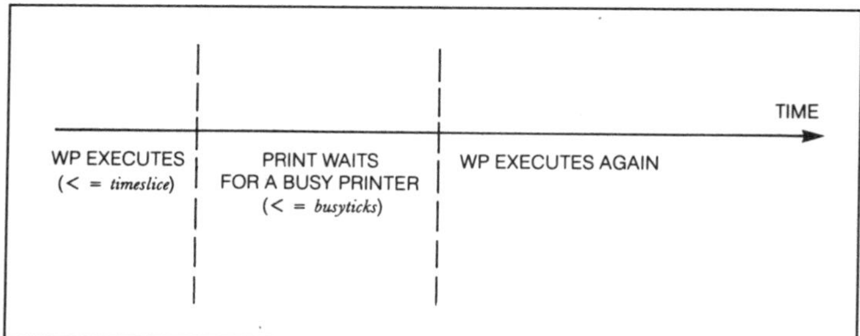

Figure 2.3: Flow of PRINT operations when the printer is busy

what happens when the printer is busy for too long a time period and *busyticks* is exceeded.

When PRINT first gains control, it checks for printer availability. If the printer remains unavailable or busy for a period of time longer than *busyticks*, control is passed immediately back to the foreground task (in this example, the word processing program). The print command forfeits the remaining time (*timeslice* minus *busyticks*).

If you have queued files for printing and wish to abort the queue selectively, you issue a PRINT *filename* /C *filename2* ... command, which cancels the file specified before the /C and all files after it, up to the next switch.

If a file is being printed, /T stops it, and DOS prints the message "All files canceled by operator" on the printer, sends a top-of-form command, and sounds the buzzer on the printer. DOS ignores anything entered on the line after a /T command.

/P has the opposite effect to the /C switch. DOS adds the file specified immediately before the /P, and all files after it, to the print queue until it encounters a /T or /C.

RESTRICTIONS

You cannot use a printer without the PRINT command once any queue begins printing. You cannot use PRINT on a network. You cannot remove the disk where the files are located from the drive until the spooler is done.

Note: *The file name is queued, not the file data. Be careful when changing a file's contents after queueing it for printing, because DOS will print the changed file, not the previous version (the version existing when the printing request was made).*

EXAMPLES

As Table 2.1 shows, you can set six switches the first time you invoke the PRINT command.

Table 2.1: Switches and parameters used for initial PRINT command only

Switch and Parameter	Effect
/D:*Device*	Specifies the device to which print output is to be sent (COM1, LPT2, and so on)
/Q:*QueueSize*	Specifies how many files can be accepted by the PRINT command at one time for background printing. Maximum number is 32, and the default value is 10
/M:*MaxTicks*	Specifies the maximum of CPU clock ticks to be used by the PRINT command each time it is given control by the CPU. Range of allowable values is 1 to 255, with a default value of 2
/B:*BufferSize*	Specifies the number of bytes in memory to be used for data to be printed. 512 bytes is standard, but it can be increased in 512-byte increments
/U:*BusyTicks*	Specifies how many clock ticks to wait for a printer that is still busy with earlier printing. Allowable range is 1 to 255, with a default value of 1
/S:*TimeSlice*	Specifies how long PRINT waits prior to getting its share of the CPU. Range is 1 to 255, with a default value of 8

For example, if you want to improve printing throughput by *max-ticks*, you enter

PRINT /M:12

This command allows six times as much time as the default value for character transmission to the printer before DOS returns control to the foreground task.

Two examples follow. The first gives maximum print time to PRINT jobs:

PRINT /M:255 /S:1 /U:255

This command virtually halts other processing tasks whenever there is printer output to manage.

The second example gives foreground processing chores high priority over printing tasks:

PRINT /M:1 /S:255 /U:1

This command allocates very little time to printing and very little time to waiting for a busy printer. To subordinate printing to any other task, it implements the maximum delay.

Table 2.2 shows the three switches you can use any time you queue files for printing with the PRINT command.

The following examples demonstrate their use. Entering

PRINT FILE*.TXT

Table 2.2: PRINT switches and parameters available at all times

Switch and Parameter	Effect
/P:*FileName(s)*	Prints the file(s) specified; this is the default
/C:*FileName(s)*	Cancels the printing of the file(s) specified
/T:*FileName(s)*	Terminates the printing of all specified file(s) in the PRINT queue

adds all the corresponding FILE⋆.TXT files to the print queue, with all of the default settings intact. The computer responds with

Name of list device [PRN]:

PRN is the default name, used here since you did not enter the /D parameter.

Entering

PRINT FILE2.TXT /C FILE3.TXT

cancels the files FILE2.TXT and FILE3.TXT from the queue.

Entering

PRINT FILEA.DAT FILE4.TXT /C FILE5.TXT FILE6.TXT /P

adds FILEA.DAT and FILE6.TXT to the queue and cancels FILE4.TXT and FILE5.TXT.

SEE ALSO

TYPE

RECOVER

RECOVER lets DOS reconstruct a file, or an entire diskful of files, that have become damaged or corrupted.

VERSION

Introduced in DOS 2.0

SYNTAX

(1) [*d:path*]**RECOVER** [*location*]*object*
(2) [*d:path*]**RECOVER** [*drive*]

d:path represents the drive and path where the command file is located if it is not in the current directory.

location represents an optional drive and path where the file *object* is located.

object represents the name, with an optional extension, of the file to be manipulated (wildcard characters may be used).

TYPE

External.

USAGE

You can recover an individual file from a disk by specifying it as the parameter of the RECOVER command. You can also use

RECOVER to attempt to recover all files on an entire disk that has gone bad. Unfortunately, results with this command are not always completely satisfactory, because many files cannot be recovered so that they can be effectively reused.

RESTRICTIONS

You cannot use RECOVER on a network disk.

EXAMPLES

Assume that your SALARY.DTA file is corrupted because of bad sectors on the disk. Use the following command to ask DOS to recover as much of the file as possible:

RECOVER SALARY.DTA

If much of the disk has gone bad, you can still ask DOS to recover as much as possible by specifying the drive letter itself:

RECOVER C:

In this example, all former file names on the disk will be replaced by a sequentially numbered series of new files. In addition, the amount of data successfully recovered will depend on how badly your disk is damaged. Executable files are usually useless after recovery; text files usually can be at least partially reconstructed with your word processor.

RENAME (REN)

The RENAME command (which can be shortened to REN) renames a file.

VERSION

Introduced in DOS 1.0

SYNTAX

REN[AME] *oldfile newfile*

oldfile	represents the optional drive and path, plus the file name and extension, of the file that will be renamed. Wildcards are allowed.
newfile	represents a new file name and extension for oldfile. Wildcards are allowed. The newfile parameter does not require or accept a prefixed drive and path.

TYPE

Internal.

USAGE

The RENAME command is often used simply to give an old file a more meaningful name, such as one that suggests the file's contents. Also, when data files are shared, a new owner may want to rename the files according to a different nomenclature. Finally, on shared systems, you may want to rename individual files to hide them from the prying eyes of other users.

RESTRICTIONS

You cannot use RENAME to give a subdirectory a new name. You cannot specify a drive for this command, and you can give a file on a particular drive a new name only on the same drive and in the same directory. Thus, you cannot type either a drive or a path in front of newfile. Attempting to use RENAME to give a file a new directory and/or drive name would be tantamount to a MOVE or COPY operation; RENAME is designed only to change the name of a file, not its physical location.

EXAMPLES

You can rename the BUDGET.TMP file as BUDGET.88 with the following command (this example assumes that the original BUDGET file appears on the data directory in the \LOTUS\DATA DIRECTORY in drive D):

```
REN D:\LOTUS\DATA\BUDGET.TMP BUDGET.88
```

BUDGET.88 still appears on the \LOTUS\DATA DIRECTORY.

A set of file names can be changed at one time by using wildcards. For example, you can change all of the accounting files that begin with the letters ACC and have the extension .NEW so that they have the extension .OLD:

```
REN ACC*.NEW ACC*.OLD
```

REPLACE

REPLACE allows easy updating of a set of files in one directory with another set (usually newer versions) in another directory or drive.

VERSION

Introduced in DOS 3.2; enhanced in DOS 4.0

SYNTAX

[*d:path*]**REPLACE** *source* [*destination*] [*switches*]

d:path represents the drive and path where the command file is located if it is not in the current directory.

source represents the optional drive and path with a mandatory file name and optional extension of the source files that will be the replacement files.

destination represents the optional drive and path of the files to be replaced.

switches represents one or more of the following:

- /A adds files.
- /P prompts you before replacing a file.
- /R replaces only read-only files on destination.
- /S replaces files anywhere in the directory structure with matching filenames.

/U	replaces files with older date and times (DOS 4 only).
/W	waits for you to insert a diskette.

TYPE

External.

USAGE

The REPLACE command is most often used for two reasons:

- To find the locations of all directories containing a particular piece of software and to replace the old versions of that software with the latest version.
- To find all of the different files in a particular directory and update each of these individual files to their latest version.

RESTRICTIONS

The /A switch is incompatible with the /S and /U switches and cannot be used in conjunction with either. The entire command line with all file specifications and all switch entries cannot exceed 63 characters.

EXAMPLES

Suppose you have acquired several software packages over the years, each of which may include its own version of COMMAND.COM. These COMMAND.COM versions may still be buried in the individual software application package directories, while your root directory contains the most current version of the DOS command interpreter.

You can upgrade all versions of the command interpreter at one time by asking DOS to replace occurrences of each version throughout the directory structure (using the /S switch) with the latest version from the system disk in drive A:

REPLACE A:\COMMAND.COM C:\ /S

Another application of REPLACE is upgrading your existing set of files with a new set from an application or system disk. For example, you might leave all current SYS files alone in your device driver directory \SYS, but add new system device drivers with the following command:

REPLACE A:*.SYS C:\SYS /A

This command leaves all existing files in the SYS directory of drive C untouched, while adding any new .SYS files from drive A to the SYS directory.

Finally, you may have a set of word-processing files stored on a diskette and wish to update your hard disk. If you have DOS 4, use the /U switch to ensure that no older files of the same name accidentally replace current versions on your hard disk. Enter

REPLACE A:*.WP C:\WP /U

In this case, only files on the diskette whose date/time of creation or last modification is more recent than the existing version on your C drive will be copied into the \WP directory on drive C.

RESTORE

RESTORE returns the original versions of files to your disks if you have properly created backup disks.

VERSION

Introduced in DOS 2.0; enhanced in DOS 3.3

SYNTAX

[*location*] RESTORE *source filespec* [*switches*]

location	represents the drive and path where the command file is located if it is not in the current directory.
source	represents the drive containing the backed up files to be restored.
filespec	represents an optional drive, path, file name, and extension of the files on the source disk to be restored. Wildcards are allowed.
switches	are any one or combination of the following:

/S	restores files in subdirectories specified in *filespec*
/P	prompts you before restoring each file if that file was modified since it was backed up.
/B:*mm-dd-yy*	restores all backed-up files that were modified on or before *mm-dd-yy*.

/A:*mm-dd-yy*	restores all backed-up files that were modified on or after *mm-dd-yy*.
/M	compares the backed-up files and the files on the destination disk and restores those files that have changed or been erased since the last backup operation.
/N	restores files that no longer exist on the destination disk.
/L:*hh-mm-ss*	restores all files changed since *hh-mm-ss*.
/E:*hh-mm-ss*	restores all files changed prior to *hh-mm-ss*.

TYPE

External.

USAGE

The RESTORE command brings files from BACKUP disks (diskettes or fixed disks) back onto a hard drive. This drive can be the original source hard drive for the files, or it can be another hard drive onto which you want to place the files.

Two switches will be useful to you at various times. If you have backed up an entire directory tree, or any subtree, you will need to use the /S switch to restore the subdirectory tree structure. Also, if you have made changes to any of the previously backed up files, you should use the /P switch to ensure that the old version does not overwrite the new version.

The /S switch performs a function similar to the /S switch of the BACKUP command. With BACKUP, the /S switch allows you to search through a directory and all its subdirectories for file names to back up. When used with RESTORE, /S ensures that the backed-up files are restored to their proper subdirectories. In fact, if DOS discovers that a subdirectory is missing during the restoration process, it will automatically recreate that directory before copying the backed-up files to it.

The /P switch is extremely important to use, especially if you're not completely sure of yourself or if much time has elapsed since the backup operation. When you specify /P, DOS will ask you during the restoration process whether you really want to restore an old version and overwrite an existing disk file. DOS will do this if the existing disk file has been updated since the earlier backup version, and if the disk file has been marked as a read-only file. Note that with RESTORE, a backup file will overwrite any existing file with the same name in the specified directory. Use the /P switch or REPLACE to avoid rewriting a file.

The /A and /B switches work similarly. The /B switch specifies the latest date by which a file can have been modified and still be eligible for restoration; the /A switch specifies the earliest date. In other words, /B restores all files changed before a certain date, while /A restores all files modified after a certain date.

The /M switch restores only files that were changed or deleted since they were backed up. For example, suppose you back up the file FILE.DAT. If you later accidentally delete it, you can restore it by specifying FILE.DAT as the name and using the /M parameter. The /N switch is similar to /M, except that it restores only files that have been deleted since they were backed up.

The /E and /L switches have the same effect as /A and /B, respectively, but refer to time, not dates.

RESTRICTIONS

Only backup files are restored. You can restore only your own shared files. Do not use RESTORE if SUBST, JOIN, or ASSIGN was invoked when a backup operation was performed.

EXAMPLES

To restore an entire hard disk from a backup set created with the BACKUP C:\ B: /S command, you enter

RESTORE B: C:*.* /S

Similarly, to restore all the word processing files backed up with the BACKUP C:\WP*.WP B: command, you enter

RESTORE B: C:\WP*.WP

SEE ALSO

REPLACE
BACKUP

SHARE

This command permits file sharing and allows you to lock a disk or all or part of a file, so that it cannot be used simultaneously by another process.

VERSION

Introduced in DOS 3.0

SYNTAX

[*d:path*]**SHARE** [**/F:***filemem*][**/L:***locks*]

d:path	represents the drive and path where the command file is located if it is not in the current directory.
/F:*filemem*	sets aside the memory to be used for keeping track of file sharing (the default value is 2048 bytes).
/L:*locks*	specifies the number of locks that can be in effect at once (the default value is 20).

TYPE

External.

USAGE

In local area networks (LANs), several users often need to access the same file for reading or writing operations. The SHARE command facilitates the necessary file sharing and locking for correct multiple access operations. Users of a DOS system connected to a LAN must invoke SHARE once to load the required code into memory.

RESTRICTIONS

You can load the SHARE command only once. Subsequent attempts at loading will yield an error message. You must reboot your computer to remove a SHARE command.

EXAMPLES

You must calculate the values for the /F and /L switches carefully. Change the default settings either to conserve space or to ensure that you have allocated enough space. Set the *filemem* switch value to the sum of 11 bytes plus the number of bytes in the full path name of each file to be shared.

Suppose that your system needs to share 50 files, each with an average full path name requiring 13 bytes (for example, /NET/DTASET01 and /NET/DTASET50). You need to allocate at least 50 × 13, or 650 bytes; rounding that number up to the next sector size suggests this SHARE command:

```
SHARE /F:1024 /L:50
```

SHARE does not prevent the use of a file by another computer when you are using networks; that kind of protection should be provided with your network software.

SORT

This command receives input, sorts it, and then passes it on for display or further manipulation.

VERSION

Introduced in DOS 2.0

SYNTAX

[*d:path*]**SORT** [/R][/ + *col*]

d:path	represents the drive and path where the command file is located if it is not in the current directory.
/R	sorts in reverse alphabetical order
/ + *col*	starts the sorting operation with column col (the default setting is column 1).

TYPE

External.

USAGE

SORT is a filter command. Data is sent in, and depending on the parameters, sorted and displayed or routed to another file. SORT can display directories in a sorted format, but it does not physically sort files on the disk.

As with FIND and MORE, the SORT command can use the redirection features of DOS to arrange data in a file. If the /R switch is used, the data is arranged line by line and sorted in either ascending order (0-9 followed by A-Z) or descending order (9-0 followed by Z-A). Using standard redirection and filtering symbols, SORT filters data from the standard input device, a file, or a pipe.

EXAMPLES

The following sequence takes the data from the PERSON.TXT file and sorts the lines in that file alphabetically, sending the results to NEWPERS.TXT:

```
SORT < PERSON.TXT >NEWPERS.TXT
```

If the important key in your file is located in any column other than the first, the /+*col* switch arranges the data according to that column. Combining /+*col* with the pipes concept, the following command arranges the directory listing of the \CAD directory according to the file extension:

```
DIR | SORT /+10
```

Sorted results are displayed on the screen. This switch can be further combined with output redirection to send a sorted directory listing (by extension) to another file.

TYPE

TYPE displays the contents of an ASCII file. ASCII files contain no control codes that affect the screen display; they appear as straight listings of data.

VERSION

Introduced in DOS 1.0

SYNTAX

Type *filespec*

filespec is the optional drive and path, plus the file name and extension, of the file to be displayed.

TYPE

Internal.

USAGE

The TYPE command is used principally to display, or type, a text file on your screen or on your printer. Using TYPE is a quick and easy way to view the contents of any text file or to obtain a quick hard copy of a small text file. (To print longer text files, use the PRINT command.)

RESTRICTIONS

Using TYPE with a non-ASCII file may have no effect, or it may display meaningless symbols on your screen. It can also lock up your system entirely. If this happens, reboot the system.

EXAMPLES

To type the file ANALYSIS.RPT on your screen, enter

TYPE ANALYSIS.RPT

To type the same file on your printer, you would use redirection techniques. Enter

TYPE ANALYSIS.RPT > PRN

SEE ALSO

PRINT

XCOPY

This command copies one or more files.

VERSION

Introduced in DOS 3.2

SYNTAX

[*d:path*]**XCOPY**
[*filespec1*][*filespec2*][**/A**][**/D:***mm-dd-yy*][**/E**][**/M**][**/P**][**/S**][**/V**][**/W**]

d:path	represents the drive and path where the command file is located if it is not in the current directory.
filespec1	represents the necessary drive, path, and filename specifications for the files to be copied. Wildcards are allowed.
filespec2	represents the necessary drive, path, and filename specifications for the files to be written to. Wildcards are allowed.
/A	copies only files with a set archive bit.
/D:*mm-dd-yy*	copies only files created or modified on or after the specified date; the date format depends on the COUNTRY specification in your CONFIG.SYS file.
/E	creates corresponding subdirectories on *filespec2* before copying (even if *filespec1* contains no files to transfer). When this switch is used, you must also select the /S switch. The /E switch controls the output end of the

	procedure (writing), and the /S switch controls the input end (reading).
/M	copies files with a set archive bit and resets the source-file archive bit.
/P	prompts you before each file is copied.
/S	copies files from all subdirectories within the specified directory. Corresponding subdirectories will be created on filespec2 for all filespec1 directories that contain files.
/V	turns verification on during execution of this command only.
/W	causes XCOPY to prompt you to insert different disks before it executes.

TYPE

External.

USAGE

XCOPY works very quickly because it reads as many source files as it can fit into memory. Only then does it begin to write the files to the destination disk. In contrast, the COPY command reads and then writes files one after the other.

Because of its speed, XCOPY should become your command of choice for transferring groups of files between directories and drives. Unfortunately, you can use it effectively only with wildcards, as it is not sophisticated enough to allow you to specify a series of separately named files.

You can combine XCOPY's switches as well. The last example in the "Examples" section uses the /S switch to traverse the directory. If you want DOS to pause and ask you to verify the copying of *each* file, you can simply add the /P switch.

RESTRICTIONS

XCOPY does not copy to or from devices. It also does not copy hidden files from the source location and will not overwrite read-only files at the destination location.

EXAMPLES

To copy all files in the \LOTUS\DATA directory of drive C to a high-capacity diskette in drive A, enter

XCOPY C:\LOTUS\DATA A:

XCOPY also can copy files from a branch of a directory tree. This means that all batch files in all directories below the root of drive D can be backed up to a diskette in drive A with the following command:

XCOPY D:*.BAT A: /S

The /S switch starts at the directory specified in *filespec1* (D:\) and works its way through all lower-level subdirectories, searching for files that meet the specification *.BAT.

SEE ALSO

BACKUP
COPY

CHAPTER 3

Hard-Disk Configuration Commands

Any programming environment can be enhanced by a variety of techniques. Some of these concentrate on the programs being used, while others concentrate on the operating system within which the programs run. DOS has a number of internal operating system variables you can control through special configuration commands. You enter these commands by including them in an ASCII text file called CONFIG.SYS, which must be located in the root directory of your boot disk. This appendix discusses only those configuration commands that, when used judiciously, can improve the overall performance of your entire DOS system. This benefit naturally spills over into the apparent performance of your individual application programs.

> ***Note:*** *None of the CONFIG.SYS file's settings take effect until the DOS system is booted. Remember, if you make any changes to your CONFIG.SYS file, you must reboot before the changes take effect.*

BUFFERS

This command causes a certain number of file-transfer buffers to be set aside in memory.

VERSION

Introduced in DOS 2; most recently enhanced in DOS 4.0

SYNTAX

BUFFERS = *x*,*y* /X

x	is the number of buffers to be set up. If this command is not specified, DOS 3.3 and later will determine the number of buffers automatically, based on the current system memory.
y	is the number of look-ahead buffers installed for reading sectors in advance during input operations (DOS 4 only).
/X	directs DOS to use expanded memory, if available, for the DOS buffers reserved by this command.

USAGE

While most programs require only a few buffers, remember that every disk access requires one. You should experiment with different values of BUFFERS, measuring your system performance using the actual program mix that you will later be running regularly. If you do not do this, or do not care what values are set for you, DOS will set BUFFERS equal to what it considers an appropriate number, as shown in Table 3.1.

The BUFFERS command refers to the way DOS manages the input and output of data to and from the disk drives. When a program issues a command to read information from a file, DOS serves the role of an intermediary by loading the information into a reserved buffer area. Figure 3.1 presents a visual interpretation of this activity.

All data that flows either to (output data) or from (input data) the disk must pass briefly through DOS's internal buffers. These are

Table 3.1: Default BUFFERS settings in DOS 3.3 and 4

System Factor	**Buffers Value**
Memory < = 128K and Disk drive < = 360K	**2**
Memory < = 128K and Disk drive > 360K	**3**
Memory < = 256K and Memory > 128K	**5**
Memory < = 512K and Memory > 256K	**10**
Memory > 512K	**15**

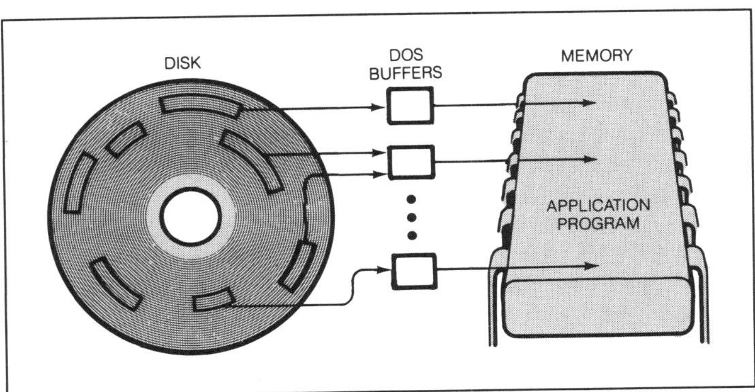

Figure 3.1: Disk data passing through DOS buffers

temporary holding places in DOS's memory space. Each buffer is 512 bytes long, and the number of available buffers has a dramatic effect on the speed of data I/O during DOS file transfers. This speed has a direct bearing on the apparent speed of application programs, particularly sophisticated programs such as data base management systems.

Efficiency is the primary reason that operating systems use buffers at all. Imagine yourself in the role of an operating system. Then imagine that someone (an application program) wants to give you something, while someone else (a disk file) wants to get that same thing. If you act as a buffer by accepting the object with one hand and then hold it until you can locate the receiving person, the transaction will be fairly straightforward. However, if you try to do this procedure without using your hands or moving around, getting the giver together with the receiver in the same room, you've made your job much more difficult. In addition, you would not be able to do much else until the two-person operation was completed. DOS uses buffers to make transactions efficient.

When DOS receives a disk request, it checks the information in its buffer before it tries to read the disk. This step can sometimes eliminate the need for DOS to actually read the disk in order to satisfy an application program's file request; DOS may find that the requested file data is already in the buffer—for example, if the file was recently called by another program or by DOS. The result is that some programs perform certain operations faster.

Each buffer in DOS consumes 528 bytes. DOS uses only 512 bytes for storing disk data; the remaining 16 bytes are used for control information to keep track of the data in the 512-byte buffer. If you increase the number of buffers, the memory-resident requirements for DOS itself increase. This decreases the available memory both for any application program and for any memory-resident program you want to use during your main program's execution. Sophisticated programs such as Framework III, which has its own buffer management and configuration file and therefore uses memory intensively, suffer greatly from too large a BUFFERS value.

The law of diminishing returns is at work here. Up to a point, more DOS buffers means faster performance for your system. On the other hand, too many buffers means DOS may spend more time looking through its buffers than it would spend going directly to the disk and reading the necessary data. Unless you have a good reason to do otherwise, use the software manufacturer's recommended setting for BUFFERS, particularly with DOS 3.3 or earlier. A common setting is a value of 15 or 20.

EXAMPLES

A common suggestion in the user manuals of various applications is to enter the following line in your CONFIG.SYS:

BUFFERS = 20

Although this sometimes works better than the default value in DOS 4, it is typically too large a number. In earlier versions of DOS, the default value was usually set too low, so this blind suggestion of a value of 20 typically improved performance. DOS's current variable default values are much better, and should usually be accepted on faith. You should change the default number only if you actually run timing tests to determine a better number for your application program mix.

A more powerful example takes into account the second parameter to this statement, available only to DOS 4 users. If you know that your primary application processes file entries in a sequential manner, you can reserve some DOS buffers for time-saving look-ahead duties. DOS will anticipate the upcoming disk I/O and fill the extra buffers with data. For example,

BUFFERS = 20,5

reserves the same 20 sectors for DOS buffers; however, this version of the command explicitly directs DOS to use up to 5 of those sectors for look-ahead efforts.

DEVICE = VDISK.SYS

This command loads the VDISK.SYS device driver, a program that enables you to create a RAM disk (or virtual disk).

VERSION

Introduced in DOS 2; enhanced in DOS 4

SYNTAX

DEVICE = [*d:path*]**VDISK.SYS**[*disk size*][*sector size*][*entries*][**/E:***max sectors*][**/X:***max sectors*]

d:path	represents the drive and path where the driver file is located if it is not in the current directory.
disk size	specifies the size in kilobytes of the virtual (RAM) disk. The value must be between 1K and the amount of available memory. If *disk size* is omitted, the default is 64K.
sector size	specifies the number of bytes in each sector of the virtual disk. Allowed values are 128, 256, and 512 bytes; the default is 128.
entries	specifies the number of directory entries the virtual disk can hold. The minimum number is 2 and the maximum is 512; the default is 64.
/E: *max sectors*	installs the virtual disk in extended memory and sets the maximum number of sectors that can be transferred to the virtual disk at once. The minimum is 1 and the maximum (and the default) is 8.

/X:*max sectors*	installs the virtual disk in expanded memory and sets the maximum number of sectors that can be transferred to the virtual disk at once. The minimum is 1 and the maximum (and the default) is 8.

USAGE

A device driver can be anything from a keyboard enhancement routine to a RAM disk specification. DEVICE can be used many times in the CONFIG.SYS file, limited only by the total available memory in the system and the amount each driver uses. Five device drivers are supplied with DOS: ANSI.SYS, VDISK.SYS, DISPLAY.SYS, PRINTER.SYS, and DRIVER.SYS. (Drivers for nonstandard devices are supplied by the device manufacturers.) One of the standard DOS drivers is of interest in the context of hard-disk management: VDISK.SYS.

When physical memory is used to simulate a mechanical disk, the resulting apparent disk drive is called a RAM disk, or virtual disk. Assuming your system has enough memory for both DOS and your main application program, the remaining memory can, in theory (it usually must be a certain minimum number of bytes, such as 256), be arranged to mimic a real disk drive. A small number of memory bytes can be used to contain directory table (DAT) information, an additional small number of bytes can be used for file allocation table (FAT) entries, and the remaining space can be used for file storage. The VDISK.SYS driver (called RAMDRIVE.SYS in MS-DOS) creates such a disk in your computer's memory.

A critical aspect of the RAM disk mechanism is that any files placed on the RAM disk are memory resident. They can therefore be retrieved at the speed of memory operations, which are usually measured in microseconds or nanoseconds. Files on actual mechanical disk drives are retrieved more slowly, usually in the millisecond range.

You must perform some calculations to determine how much memory is available for your RAM disk. Simply subtract the memory required by your version of DOS from your total physical memory (640K, 512K, or whatever). Then subtract the memory required by your largest application program (for example, 384K for XYWRITE or 512K for CADVANCE) from the remaining number. This tells you the maximum remaining memory space you can allocate for a RAM disk. For example, if the total physical memory of your system is 640K, the space required by your DOS 4 is 70K, and the space required by your application program is 384K, you have 186K remaining for your RAM disk (640 − 70 − 384 = 186).

There are a few other factors you must consider. The size of your version of DOS varies according to the values of FILES, BUFFERS, and any other CONFIG.SYS parameters. It also varies according to how many additional DOS programs that require extra memory you've run (for example, the MODE or APPEND commands). Naturally, if you run a memory-resident programs such as Sidekick, you need to subtract its memory requirements as well.

Use only as much memory for your RAM disk as you need. You should know in advance how you plan to use this space. Keep in mind that memory reserved for use as a RAM disk is no longer available for internal use by programs such as Framework III or Symphony. If a RAM disk or any other memory-resident software uses too much space, you may not have even enough remaining memory to load your main application software.

Now that you know how to create a RAM disk, you should also learn how to use what you've created to best advantage. Here are some suggestions for using your RAM disk.

- Copy your DOS system's primary disk-resident program, COMMAND.COM, onto your RAM disk. Then employ the following special instructions to inform DOS that all future references to COMMAND.COM refer to the copy on the RAM disk, not on the boot disk. Assuming your RAM disk is in drive D (substitute the letter used by your system), enter the following command at the DOS prompt:

  SET COMSPEC = D:\COMMAND.COM

  This will speed up all programs that invoke DOS from within themselves, such as Framework III or Q-DOS II. These programs work by loading a second copy of the command processor (COMMAND.COM) from a RAM disk. This command will also speed up application software that overwrites the command-processor portion of DOS and then requires its reloading before the software can restore DOS and its prompt.

The SET command enables users to define and later modify variables, like COMSPEC, that are stored in a reserved memory area called the DOS environment. All commands, functions, and application programs can access the string variables stored in the DOS environment, making it an excellent tool for sharing common data across applications, thereby facilitating sophisticated techniques such as this one used by VDISK.SYS.

- Load the files for frequently referenced external DOS commands, such as CHKDSK.COM and FORMAT.COM, onto your RAM disk; also load EDLIN.COM if you use EDLIN often to edit small text files. In fact, load any text files, such as batch files, that you run frequently.
- Load any large support files (such as spelling dictionaries or a thesaurus file) that your word processor or integrated software may need. Also place index-type files (generated by many database management systems) on the RAM disk to access data records much more rapidly, especially if you must search through many records in large data files.
- Place your favorite disk-resident utility programs (shareware, public domain, or purchased, such as the Norton Utilities) on the RAM disk if you use them frequently.
- Also place overlay files on your RAM disk for improved execution of your software. These overlays contain the portion of your application program that couldn't fit into memory and is normally read into a special part of memory only when it is needed. The overlay features of your software will operate at rapid RAM speeds if you place them on your RAM disk. Note that you will need to make your RAM disk the default DOS disk before invoking your application program, so DOS will look for the overlay file on the RAM disk and not on the standard drive.
- Remember to set your path properly so DOS can find main programs. Set the RAM disk near or at the front of the PATH specification so that DOS first accesses the file copies on the RAM drive, not the original files that may also be accessible from directories on the path.

Before you follow these suggestions for using your RAM disk effectively, you should learn how to use it safely. As you know, using a RAM disk is much faster than using real disks. Programs that formerly took hours to run may take minutes, those that took minutes may take seconds, and waiting time may disappear. When RAM disks are used improperly, however, hours of work can disappear in seconds.

Since a RAM disk is created in memory, any information stored on it will vanish when the computer is turned off. You gain great advantage by storing and accessing the right files on a RAM disk, but you must remember that these files are destroyed when you turn off the power or a power failure occurs, if your computer plug comes out of the wall, or if you reboot your system with Ctrl-Alt-Del.

If you place and update important data files on a RAM disk for the sake of rapid access, save copies of them on a real disk before you turn off the power. Also make backup copies of them on a real disk at frequent intervals to avoid losing all your work.

EXAMPLES

> ***Note:*** *If you are using a version of DOS for any machine other than an IBM computer, you will need to substitute RAMDRIVE.SYS wherever VDISK.SYS appears in the following examples.*

The simulated RAM disk in Figure 3.2 can be implemented simply by including a line like the following in your DEVICE specification:

DEVICE = C:\DOS\VDISK.SYS 120

This DEVICE setting brings into memory the VDISK driver. In this example, the VDISK.SYS file itself is located on drive C in the DOS directory. The parameter value of 120 indicates that a total simulated disk of 120K should be created from the available physical memory (640K or whatever you have in your system). In practice, the size you allocate would depend on the factors discussed earlier.

If you have an IBM PC-AT or a compatible computer, you should know about a switch you can use when you set up a RAM disk. The

/E switch will use extended memory—extra memory above the conventional 1Mb of addressible memory—if your machine has this additional memory installed. Since many DOS application programs do not use any memory beyond 640K, using extended memory is an excellent idea. Not only do you retain low memory for your programs but you are not as limited in the size of the RAM disk you can create. The previous example could be modified as follows to generate a 120K RAM disk in extended memory:

DEVICE = C:\DOS\VDISK.SYS 120 /E

DOS also allows you to use multiple RAM disks simultaneously, just as you can use different physical devices to protect files from one another by separating them on different drives. DOS will give each RAM disk a new single-character drive identifier.

All you need to do to create multiple RAM disks is enter multiple copies of the DEVICE command. DOS knows what physical drives exist in your system, and it creates the additional drives using the next available letters. For instance, if your system has two diskette drives and one hard-disk drive, adding the following two statements to your CONFIG.SYS file would create RAM disks D and E with sizes of 120K and 184K:

DEVICE = C:\DOS\VDISK.SYS 120
DEVICE = C:\DOS\VDISK.SYS 184

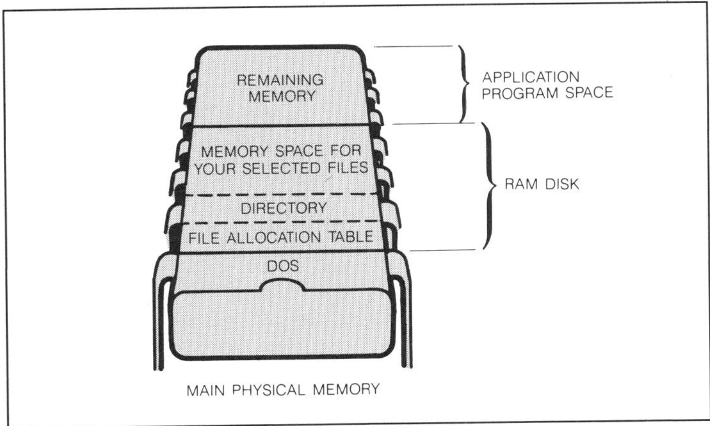

Figure 3.2: RAM disk simulation using physical memory

If you intend to create and use disk drives with drive identifiers beyond the letter E, DOS 3.2 through 4 will permit you to do so but will require another statement in your configuration file. This additional statement must be of the form LASTDRIVE=x, where x is the last valid alphabetic character DOS will use for a drive identifier (see LASTDRIVE later in this chapter).

SEE ALSO

LASTDRIVE

FCBS

In DOS version 1, files were accessed via file control blocks (FCBs). These are approximately 40-byte sections in memory that tell DOS a file's name and other attributes. The FCBS command allows you to access FCBs.

VERSION

Introduced in DOS 3.0

SYNTAX

FCBS = *maxnum,permnum*

maxnum	is the number of FCBs that may be opened concurrently (the default value is 4).
permnum	is the minimum number of FCBs that will remain open when DOS tries to close files automatically (the default value is 0).

USAGE

Very few application environments require the inclusion of an FCBS entry in your CONFIG.SYS. However, if you are still using an old program, or an early version of a current program, and the documentation advises an FCBS entry, you have no choice but to include the proper line.

RESTRICTIONS

If *permnum* is less than *maxnum*, DOS can close an FCB without alerting the program that is using the FCB, an operation that can cause major problems.

EXAMPLES

If your application program uses the older-style file control blocks to maintain status and structure for open files, you must include an FCBS command in your CONFIG.SYS file. For example,

```
FCBS=10,6
```

initializes DOS to allow up to 10 files to be opened concurrently using the file control block method. Six of these files will be kept open at all times. If an application attempts to open 13 files, DOS will keep the first 6 open, and may close 3 of the next 4 that were opened in order to open the eleventh, twelfth, and thirteenth files referenced.

FILES

Just as the number of buffers to be used by DOS can be specified, so may the number of files open at any one time. The FILES command specifies the size of the file control area in which file control blocks are created. Once again, this number shouldn't be set any higher than needed for the number of files required to be open by your application program mix. This is because when you are using the FILES command, the size of DOS increases by 48 bytes for each file control block set beyond the default value of eight files.

VERSION

Introduced in DOS 2.0.

SYNTAX

FILES = x

x	represents a number between 8 and 255 (8 is the default) specifying the number of files that can remain open at one time.

USAGE

Why is this statement necessary at all? More and more frequently, users are running sophisticated programs, such as XYWRITE III PLUS, dBASE IV, and Framework III, that can work with a number of files open at the same time. The FILES entry in the CONFIG.SYS file allows you to change the normal DOS default value for the maximum number of allowable files to be simultaneously in use.

The default value set by DOS is only eight files. This means that DOS reserves eight places inside its own memory space to track information about open files. DOS itself uses three of these places, and every running application program, overlay file, RAM-resident program, and so on may use additional places out of the eight.

EXAMPLES

Most popular application programs recommend that you set the FILES value to 20 in your CONFIG.SYS file, although some programs recommend higher or lower settings:

```
FILES=20
```

Unless you're willing to run extensive performance tests in your system environment, just follow the software manufacturer's instructions for setting the value of FILES. However, if you are using several different software application packages—for example, you may be using a computer-aided design package that recommends the setting FILES=20, and you may also be using a database management package that recommends FILES=15—use the largest suggested value. Although doing so will cost you some additional memory space when DOS boots up, the cost won't be excessive (48 bytes per open file). In nearly all cases, using the larger value will ensure that all of the application packages perform efficiently. Very occasionally, the extra table setting—say, of five files (20 − 15) —will take up just enough memory to inhibit one of the application programs from running. When this happens (usually only in systems with less than 640K, or in systems using several additional memory-resident software programs), you will need to use a different version of your CONFIG.SYS file for each of the different application programs.

LASTDRIVE

This command allows you to specify up to 26 disk drives for access. If you actually have several different physical disk drives, this command is essential. However, you may choose to partition your hard disk into several logical drives (see the FDISK program in Appendix D). In this case, you can arrange your work and files cleanly onto completely different disk drives; this can be beneficial to segmenting different projects or different users of the same hardware.

VERSION

Introduced in DOS 3.2.

SYNTAX

LASTDRIVE=*d*

d	represents the last accessible drive; the default is E.

USAGE

Using RAM disks may require that you use this command. So will using a variety of logical drives caused by partitioning, and preparing those logical drives in an extended DOS partition. If you have more than five drives hooked up to your system, or if you are using the SUBST command often and need to declare a drive name beyond E, you also need to use this command. LASTDRIVE configures the system so that you can access drives up to the specified drive, which may even be Z.

RESTRICTIONS

If you specify a letter range that is not sufficient for the number of drives hooked up to the system, LASTDRIVE will not be accepted. For example, if you specify G as the final drive and have eight drives hooked up to your system, LASTDRIVE will not work—you've assigned only seven letters to cover your eight drives.

EXAMPLES

Since DOS automatically adjusts for drive letters up to the letter E, you needn't concern yourself about LASTDRIVE in a typical system. However, your system may have two 5¼-inch diskette drives (A and B), a 70Mb hard disk with a primary DOS partition of 20Mb used as the boot drive (C), an extended partition on the 70Mb drive split up into two 25Mb logical drives (D and E), and a 3½-inch 1.44Mb microfloppy drive (F). In this system, you would need to include the following line in your CONFIG.SYS file:

LASTDRIVE = F

SEE ALSO

DEVICE
FDISK
SUBST

Part II

Exploring the Benefits of Third-Party Utilities

Microsoft supplies many useful programs with DOS; as with all things, however, there is still room for improvement. In this Part, you will learn about what I consider to be the best examples of improvements to DOS.

Thousands of utility programs are available today; advertisements for such products appear in all major personal computer magazines. In these chapters, you will discover why the Norton Utilities has been the premier hard-disk utility package for years, why Q-DOS II is the best hard disk manager around, and why Back-It can save you great amounts of backup time on a regular basis.

CHAPTER 4

Managing Your Disk Contents with The Norton Utilities

DOS offers third party utility developers many opportunities to either improve on the built in command set or to fill in where DOS does not provide functionality. In the next three chapters, you will discover what I consider the most useful add-on utility programs for hard disk management. The Norton Utilities is a sophisticated set of useful utility programs designed to increase your control over the data stored on your disk. For example, you can look at specific parts of a disk and modify the data you find there. You can also recover files that have been accidentally erased; you can even recover entire hard disks that have been reformatted. Utilities of this kind come in very handy when you've made a major blunder. Even if things are going smoothly, the Norton Utilities can provide you with a greater understanding of how your system is set up, as well as an insider's glimpse into previously inaccessible disk files.

The Norton Utilities package has some significant benefits for hard-disk users. The following list contains the primary utility functions of interest to hard disk users. It is not a comprehensive list of all the Norton utilities:

- In the latest version of the Norton Utilities, you access all the program's features through a single controlling menu program, called the Norton Integrator (NI.EXE). This program enables you to run any of the other utility programs. It shows the syntax of each utility, including a brief explanation of the parameters and switch options.

- The NU utility offers convenient access to and modification capability for any byte on your disk, by directory and file, as well as by cluster and sector. This utility enables you to recover nearly all of a deleted file whose disk space has been partially reused by DOS.
- The QU program provides you with the easy and quick ability to reverse the devastating effects of inadvertent file erasure.
- The FR utility offers a similar ability on a grander scale. It enables you to recover all files on a disk that has been accidentally formatted.
- The DT utility provides a facility for checking the physical integrity of a disk. You also gain the opportunity to repair, correct, move, and mark damaged sectors.
- The LP utility offers an occasionally useful printing capability. For those of you who have to print out programs or files for books, manuals, or reports, the strength of this utility lies in its ability to prepare a text file for printing in a variety of ways, most particularly with line numbers. This can save you the trouble of editing the file for the sole purpose of the line numbered printout.

The most current version of the Norton Utilities is available in two forms: Standard version 4.5 and Advanced version 4.5. The difference can be significant. The Advanced version includes all utilities from the standard version plus the special-purpose Speed Disk (SD) and Format Recover (FR) programs. Furthermore, the Advanced version includes what is known as the "Disk Doctor," which facilitates manipulation of absolute physical sectors, as well as the editing of directory, FAT, and partition table entries.

The Norton Utilities package is available from:

Peter Norton Computing, Inc.
2210 Wilshire Boulevard, Suite 186
Santa Monica, California 90403
(213) 453-2361
(213) 319-2000

Using the Norton Integrator Menu

The Norton Integrator, NI.EXE, is all you have to remember once you've loaded the entire Norton Utilities onto your hard disk and set your PATH to them properly. Figure 4.1 shows the standard results of entering

NI

at your DOS prompt, or executing NI from the File System window of DOS 4. The left column of the screen lists the names of the various Norton Utilities; you need only move the cursor to the desired utility to see a screenful of information about it. In Figure 4.1, the cursor has been moved down to the fourth utility, the Disk Test. As you highlight each utility name, the right window of the screen fills in with a brief description of the program, its formal syntax, its possible parameters and switches, and occasionally some advice on usage. More detailed context-sensitive help is always available by pressing F1. Each highlighted choice is replicated on the bottom line of the Integrator screen. You can press ↵ to initiate the program immediately, or you can first type in any desired parameters and switch values, and then press ↵.

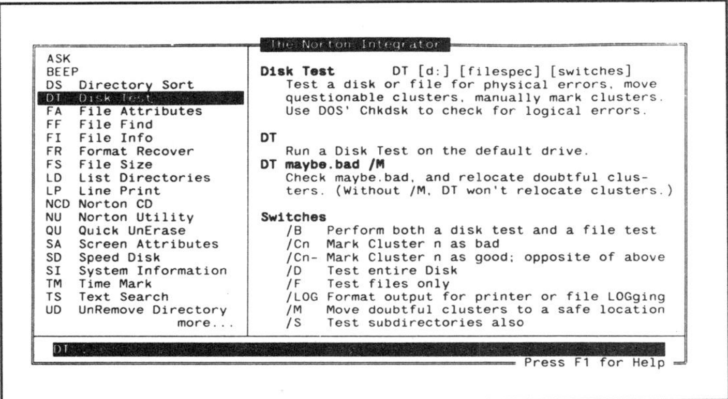

Figure 4.1: The Norton Integrator Screen

Following are brief discussions of the most important programs in the Norton Utilities.

Disk Test The Disk Test utility is good to use on a regular basis with your hard disk(s) and comes in handy for rapid validation of diskettes that begin to have occasional problems. This utility reads your disk, either file by file or cluster by cluster, to determine if any read errors occur. You are informed of any cluster numbers that exhibit problems, and whether those clusters are currently in use by one of your files. If errors appear, it is time to attempt to save the data in the affected files, or to consider moving all unaffected files to a new disk. The utility also allows you to mark the affected sectors as bad, thereby eliminating the possibility of future use by DOS for some other file data.

Format Recover The Format Recover utility, selected in Figure 4.2, may never be necessary. When used, it can completely restore a hard disk that has lost all its directory structure and file data due to accidental reformatting. However, it's so simple to include a line, such as

FR C: /SAVE

in your AUTOEXEC.BAT file that it's unreasonable not to do so.

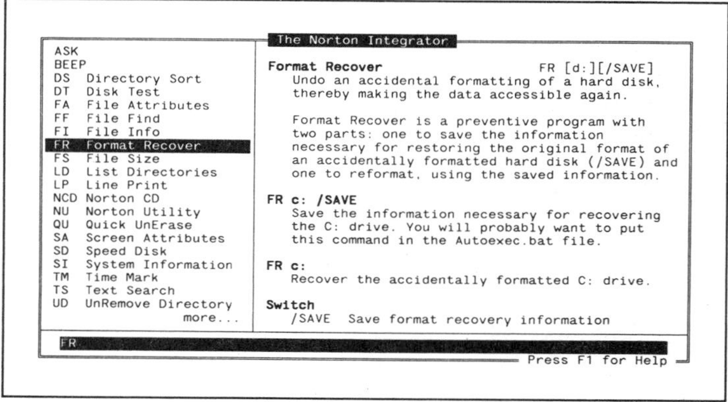

Figure 4.2: Recovering a formatted disk with FR

Using the SAVE switch will save the required information in a recoverable location. In this way, an accidentally formatted disk can be easily recovered by merely running the FR utility again and specifying the disk drive identifier:

FR C:

This command will restore the original disk formatting, as well as all the files as they existed at the time the FR utility was last run using the /SAVE switch.

File Size The File Size utility (see Figure 4.3) gives you a quick report of the space taken up by a specified group of files. The FS utility can also be used to determine whether the files specified can fit on a target drive, a helpful feature if you are writing files to a diskette already containing other files.

FS is also used simply to display the size of various disk files. Since disk space is allocated by clusters, there is often wasted space at the end of a file. This difference between required space (amount actually needed by your application) and allocated space (amount assigned by DOS through the file system's algorithm) is called *slack*. The FS utility can detail the amount of individual slack in files, as well as the amount in separate directories, and on entire disks.

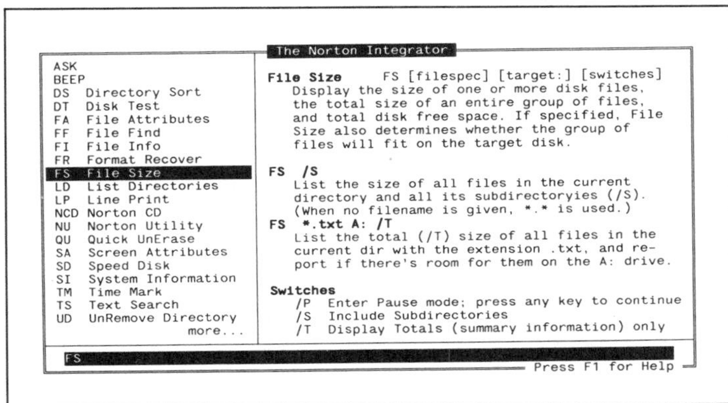

Figure 4.3: The File Size Utility

Line Print The Line Print utility, LP.EXE, provides the wide range of switch options seen in Figure 4.4. Any text file can be formatted for output printing, with switch settings controlling margins, spacing, character set, line numbering, and so on. Its major advantage is that the formatting takes place at the time of output, requiring no effort to edit the text file itself. When you are preparing programming language files for this type of printout, you can continue to deal with the actual program file, rather than having to create a separate file for printing purposes only.

Authors of papers, books, and articles use this utility all the time. Although any word processor allows you to create the same type of formatted output, using such a program requires you to edit the actual data file for the purposes of printing. The LP utility provides a wide range of switch options that can modify the formatted output without affecting the original file. And this modification takes no effort on your part; it occurs during the operation of the LP utility which then produces a formatted output report, display, or file.

All programmers can make effective use of this utility for documenting their code. The actual code files can remain untouched, while separate files can be prepared by LP containing headers, line and page numbers, and adjusted page and margin sizes. Programmers particularly will appreciate the ability to use LP to send setup strings out to the printer to influence the final appearance of the printout, taking into account any special features of that printer.

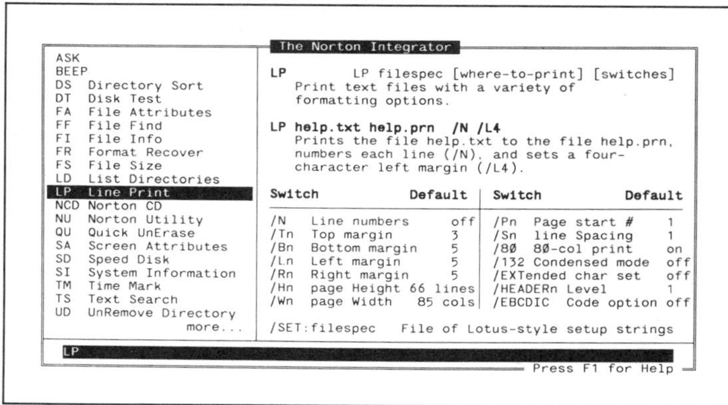

Figure 4.4: The Line Print Utility

Norton Utility The NU utility is probably the best known of all the Norton Utilities. It provides the most extensive and sophisticated features for investigating, managing, and modifying any and all data information on your hard disk. Figure 4.5 shows the first of many possible screens displayed by this full screen utility program.

When you use the NU utility, the bottom of the screen always displays the current drive, directory, filename, and file type being analyzed or modified in the central window portion of the screen. The various menu possibilities are extensive. For instance, selecting *Explore disk* from the screen shown in Figure 4.5 results in the screen shown in Figure 4.6. At this point, you can select a different directory, a different disk drive, or a different file. For that matter, if you know the precise cluster or sector number you are interested in, you can even specify those values in particular. Full screen graphic directory trees are in vogue, being the most common presentation method here (see Figure 4.7) as well as in Q-DOS II (see Chapter 5) and in DOS 4's TREE command itself (see Chapter 1).

Once a directory has been selected, you can select a particular file or subdirectory from a full screen list presented to you by another menu choice. At any time, your current choices for drive, directory, and file become the subject of any action you select. For instance, selecting *Information on item* from the screen shown in Figure 4.6

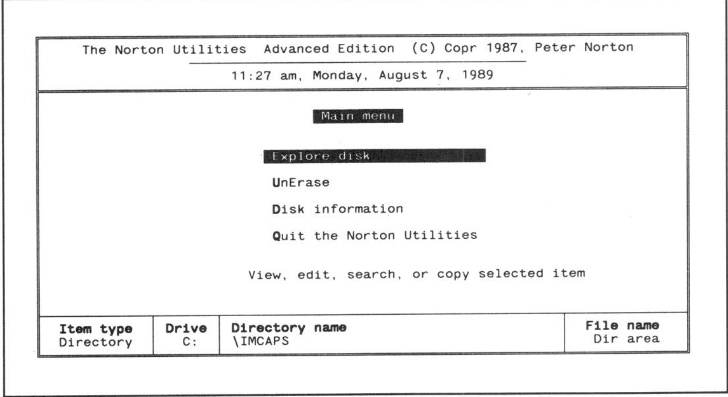

Figure 4.5: The Norton Utilities principal program, NU.EXE

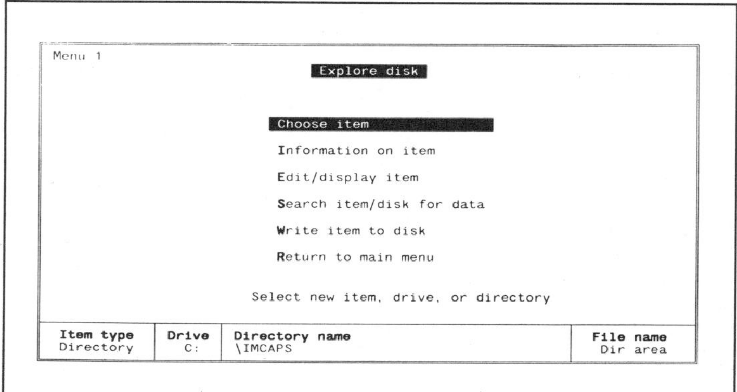

Figure 4.6: The NU Explore Disk submenu

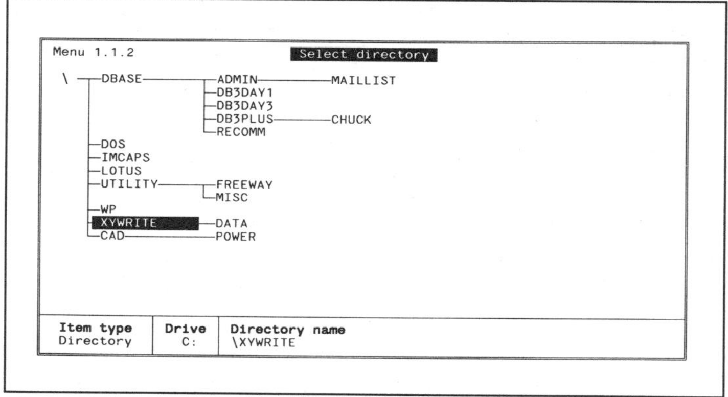

Figure 4.7: Selecting a new directory in the NU utility

might produce the display about the selected EDITOR.EXE file shown in Figure 4.8.

Selecting Disk information from the screen shown in Figure 4.5 might produce the proportional disk map shown in Figure 4.9. This provides the clearest visual evidence of the extent of your hard disk's fragmentation. The more gaps that are evident in your disk's cluster allocations, the more time DOS must spend in locating and accessing file information, and the slower your system will become. You

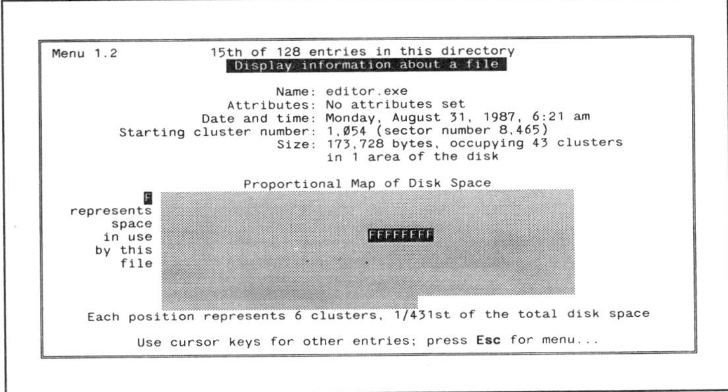

Figure 4.8: Information about the selected EDITOR.EXE file

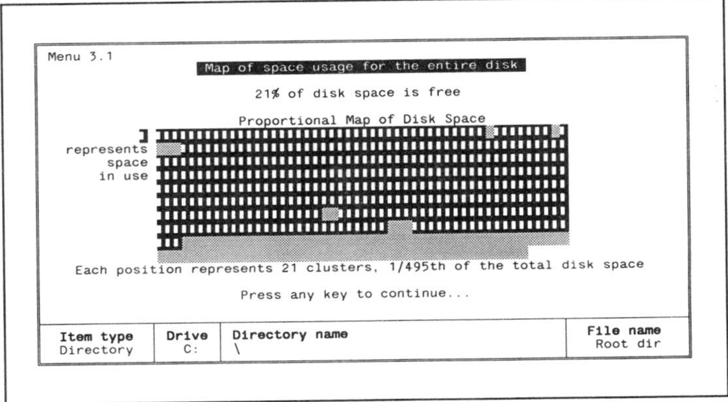

Figure 4.9: Proportional map of overall disk space usage

should periodically use this screen to assess the degree of fragmentation on your hard disk(s). When the scattering becomes visibly significant, then it is time to use Norton's Speed Disk (SD) utility, described later in this section.

All of the methods discussed in this chapter for accessing information on your hard disk work well when you know where to look. The NU utility, however, will also hunt for you if you don't know where to go. You can select *Search item/disk* for data on the screen shown in

Figure 4.6 to receive the inquiry screen shown in Figure 4.10. This example shows the letters IBM as the search characters. You can enter them as either ASCII characters or their Hexadecimal equivalents; both are displayed for you as you enter the characters. You can control on a Where to search menu whether the character search is to proceed across the entire disk, the data area only, the space occupied by erased files, or simply the currently selected item.

Once the characters have been found, you can display the sector containing the characters. Figure 4.11 shows a typical hexadecimal format display, showing hex codes on the left, and ASCII equivalents on the right. The sectors shown here are precisely those occupied by the CONFIG.SYS file; it may be seen in a standard ASCII display form in Figure 5.3, as shown by Q-DOS II in the next chapter.

The NU utility includes many other features that can't be covered in this chapter. One last capability that we will cover is the sophisticated data recovery mechanism for repairing damaged disks and files. If you've lost an important and very large file, and part of its data clusters have been reused by DOS for another file, the advanced recovery mechanism available in NU may be your only means of recovering most of the file.

You can run the NU utility for advanced file recovery by selecting NU from the main Norton Integrator menu (see Figure 4.3). By using the /M switch, you can even modify physical disk sectors without passing through DOS's file management logic. In this way,

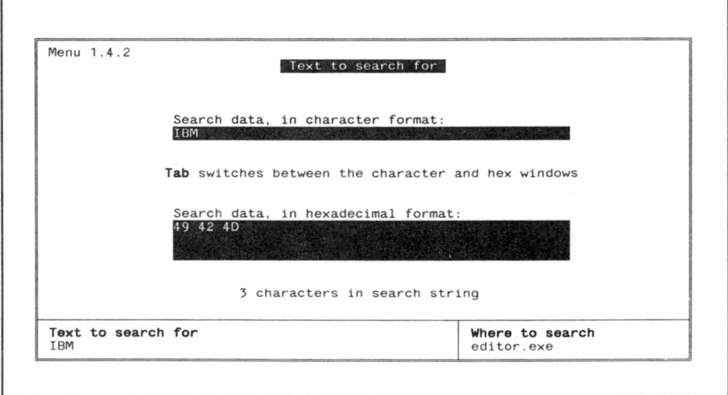

Figure 4.10: Searching for specific character strings

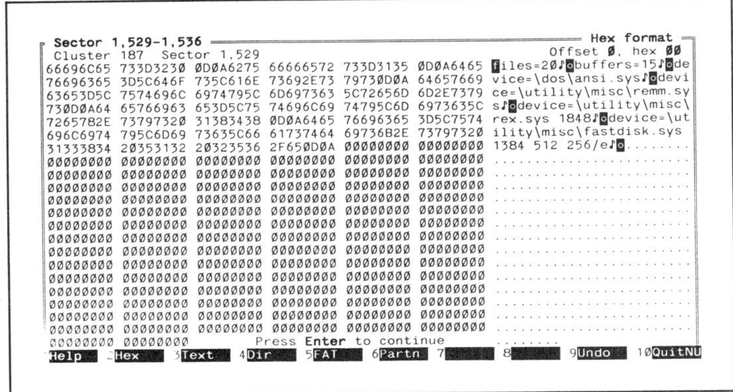

Figure 4.11: Typical NU hexadecimal display of sector information

the utility will enable you to fix errors on disks that are otherwise too scrambled to even get to with DOS's normal access (through the File Allocation Table). We won't cover this unusually advanced technique here; we will concentrate on the more typical recovery of files that have been completely or partially lost from your hard disk.

The advanced file recovery logic is accessible by selecting *Unerase* from the main menu seen in Figure 4.5. Making this choice lets you select the drive or directory containing the erased file and then to actually select which file to reconstruct. After selecting the desired drive and directory (on screens similar to the one seen in Figure 4.7), you receive a display like that seen in Figure 4.12.

The listing seen contains all deleted files; these are the candidates for restoration. In this example, only one file name appears. Any additional possibilities would be displayed in the scrolling center window of this screen.

The first question asked by NU after a file is selected for unerasure is the character to be used in place of the displayed question mark (?). This symbol is used to indicated a deleted filename. Entering the letter *j*, for example, displays the next screen in this recovery process, shown in Figure 4.13.

This recovery menu displays all of the principal choices you now have for reconstructing your file. You can leave recovery processing to Norton's automatic algorithm, or you can look at individual sectors and clusters in order to select the data for your reconstructed

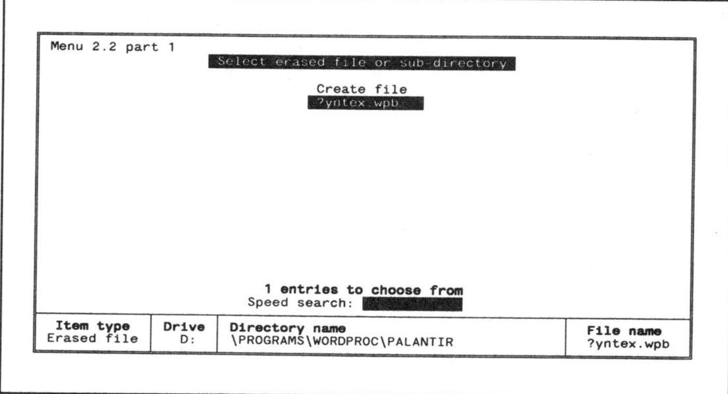

Figure 4.12: List of possible files to recover.

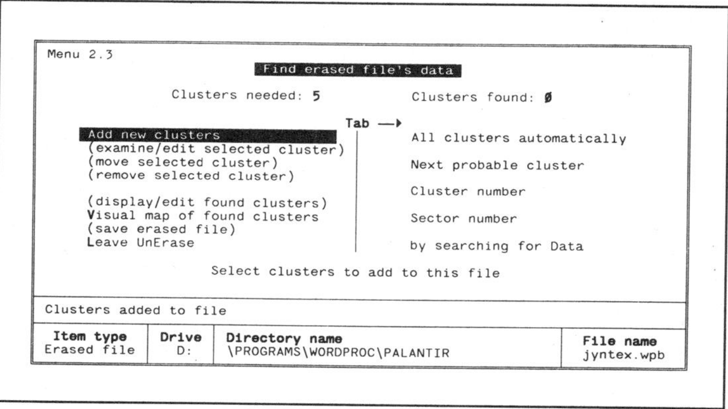

Figure 4.13: Primary recovery screen for NU Unerase.

file. You can even ask NU to search the entire disk for uniquely specified characters as an aid to locating the sectors to be included in the reconstructed file.

Quick Unerase Norton Utilities includes a simpler unerase utility, the QU.EXE program. If DOS has not reused any of the data clusters associated with a deleted file, QU can recover it in moments. As Figure 4.14 indicates, an erased file has only the first

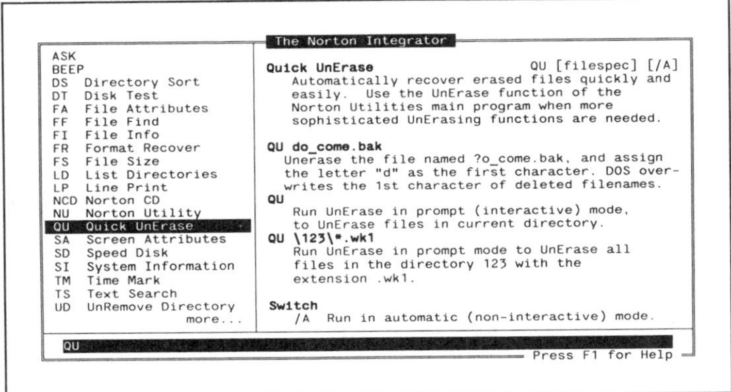

The Norton Integrator
ASK
BEEP
DS Directory Sort
DT Disk Test
FA File Attributes
FF File Find
FI File Info
FR Format Recover
FS File Size
LD List Directories
LP Line Print
NCD Norton CD
NU Norton Utility
QU Quick UnErase
SA Screen Attributes
SD Speed Disk
SI System Information
TM Time Mark
TS Text Search
UD UnRemove Directory
more...
Quick UnErase QU [filespec] [/A]
Automatically recover erased files quickly and easily. Use the UnErase function of the Norton Utilities main program when more sophisticated UnErasing functions are needed.
QU do_come.bak
Unerase the file named ?o_come.bak, and assign the letter "d" as the first character. DOS over-writes the 1st character of deleted filenames.
QU
Run UnErase in prompt (interactive) mode, to UnErase files in current directory.
QU \123*.wk1
Run UnErase in prompt mode to UnErase all files in the directory 123 with the extension .wk1.
Switch
/A Run in automatic (non-interactive) mode.
QU
Press F1 for Help

Figure 4.14: The Quick Unerase utility

character of its filename replaced to indicate its erasure. The data sectors have not been affected. This comes in handy after accidental erasures, or after you've simply had a change of mind about the importance of an erased file.

The QU utility is easily invoked from the Norton Integrator screen. QU presents each deleted file, and asks you to replace the question mark with a desired letter in the first character position of each file you want to recover. If no files can be quickly unerased with this method, you are told as much, and the utility ends. If you know that you wish to recover all possible files in a particular directory, you can invoke QU with the /A switch. This then switches QU into automatic mode. Instead of stopping to ask you if you want to recover each file or not, then asking you for the desired letter, it simply requests the replacement letter, saving one step and therefore time.

Speed Disk One last utility operation is important to discuss. The Speed Disk utility (SD) can make the arrangement of and access to your file data more efficient. If you have a hard-disk system, the efficient operation of the disk is crucial to the efficient use of your entire computer system. As the number of files on your hard disk gets larger, the time required to access a file increases, slowing down your system. There are several reasons for this slowdown, but first and foremost is a process called *fragmentation.*

When DOS writes a file on a disk, it writes it in groups of sectors called clusters. The number of 512-byte sectors in each cluster varies depending on the version of DOS you are using, but the process of cluster writing creates the speed problem. For example, suppose that you write a first file to a disk, and it consumes a full cluster. Then you write another file to the disk, and it uses up the next (contiguous) cluster. Your disk looks like this:

CLUSTER	CONTENTS
1	File 1 (first cluster of file 1)
2	File 2 (first cluster of file 2)

Then you double the size of the first file, perhaps by expanding a database or adding text with your word processor; you then save it again. Instead of pushing the second file up to make room for the two clusters of the first file, DOS saves the additional information for the first file in cluster 3, leaving cluster 2, which contains the second file, untouched. If you were to expand the second file next and then add a third file, the disk would look like this:

CLUSTER	CONTENTS
1	File 1 (first cluster of file 1)
2	File 2 (first cluster of file 2)
3	File 1 (second cluster of file 1)
4	File 2 (second cluster of file 2)
5	File 2 (third cluster of file 2)
6	File 3 (first cluster of file 3)
.	.
.	.
.	.

As you can see, files get broken up as you work on them. The time it takes to move the disk's read/write head can increase dramatically as the number of your files increases and as your files become more and more fragmented. Fragmentation occurs when pieces of the same file are stored in nonadjacent clusters on a disk. As this condition evolves, the first half of a file could be on an outside track, whereas the second half could be on an inside track. Head movement across the disk would take a lot more time than it would with sequential clusters.

Reducing or eliminating fragmentation speeds up the disk. The way to do this is to go through the whole disk and rearrange the clusters so that all clusters for every file are contiguous. With a great deal of effort, you can actually do this yourself. All you need to do is copy all files in all directories onto backup disks, reformat the entire disk, and then rewrite the files back onto the disk. An easier procedure is to use the SD utility in the Norton package.

The intention of this utility is not only to reduce fragmentation by compacting (and eliminating) unused sectors, but also to relocate files. By placing files near the directory entries that reference them, Norton expects to reduce eventual disk-head movement experienced in obtaining access to those files. In practice, however, this approach results in a time-consuming process of defragmentation, and causes many well meaning computer users to avoid using the SD utility at all.

Other Norton Utilities All the remaining utilities are interesting and useful. However, if you follow the advice of this book, you'll wind up purchasing Q-DOS II, which provides many of the same features in a slightly different format. When two separate programs provide the same features, it sometimes becomes a question of style only as to which is better. For utilities such as File Attributes (FA) and File Find (FF), I prefer the method used by Q-DOS II, presented in the next chapter. Other utilities, such as Time Mark (TM) or UnRemove Directory (UD), are useful only occasionally. They fall into the category that many blades on a multi-purpose pocket knife fall into: psychologically nice to have but not necessary for survival.

Personally, I use all the Norton Utilities except for Speed Disk. Reducing fragmentation on a regular basis is very important, but I've chosen a significantly faster utility to do so. VOPT provides a package of utilities, but its central gem is a utility that defragments hard disks rapidly. It's so fast that I include it in my AUTOEXEC.BAT file so that my disk fragmentation is minimized each time I boot up.

Tips on Using the Norton Utilities

Some tips and tricks can be employed to use the various utilities included in the Norton Utilities package more effectively.

- You can sort all files on your hard disk quickly by using the Directory Sort utility, as in **DS N \ /S**, which arranges by name all files in all directories beginning at the root.
- Use the Disk Test utility to determine if any files contain bad clusters. You should use the cluster-move capability to reduce the likelihood of data loss and increase the likelihood of data recovery.
- Include the Format Recover command, with the /SAVE switch, in your AUTOEXEC.BAT file. Do it today!
- Unless you have a photographic memory, use the Norton Integrator program. Its built-in help function and constant display of possible switches and parameter options give you easy access to the power of all the Norton Utilities.
- If your hard disk ever becomes damaged beyond apparent recall, enter the NU utility from a diskette version, specifying the special Maintenance (/M) mode. Although you won't be able to access files or directories, you can still access individual clusters and sectors.
- Always try to recover deleted files with the QU utility first. If this doesn't work, then try the advanced methods for partial file recovery contained in the NU program.

CHAPTER 5

Improving Your Hard Disk Management with Q-DOS II

Managing many directories on a hard disk can require great effort and care. However, a class of utility programs best described as hard-disk organizers can relieve your burden. In this chapter, you'll look at one such program, Q-DOS II, which can greatly simplify your task of tracking and accessing a complex tree structure of directories and files on your hard disk.

Q-DOS II has some significant benefits, compared both to DOS and to similar utility programs:

- Q-DOS II is faster than competitive hard-disk organizers. For many people, this feature may be sufficient to select Q-DOS II as your hard-disk management program.
- The convenient visual tree display works well to enable you to make, remove, and change directories easily.
- Finding, viewing, and printing files are major selection options on Q-DOS II's main menu. These choices reduce the overall keystrokes and time required to perform similar functions under DOS.
- Multiple files may be easily selected and then acted on by standard commands such as Copy, Erase, and Rename. This is a major improvement over DOS 3 capabilities, and is comparable to the graphic selection mechanism available in DOS 4.

- Multiple files may be moved extremely rapidly from one directory to another. Although DOS 4 contains this feature (DOS 3.31 and earlier do not), the DOS approach is a time-consuming copy/delete combination, whereas the Q-DOS II approach is a more sophisticated and much faster rewriting of directory entries.
- You can configure Q-DOS II to use either its built-in text editor or your own favorite word processing program. Once you've done so, you can select text files and begin editing them with a single keystroke. In my opinion, it is a great advantage to have a configuring feature that allows you to tie your own favorite word processor into Q-DOS II's menu scheme.

Q-DOS II is available from:

Gazelle Systems
42 North University Avenue, Suite 10
Provo, Utah 84601
(800) 233-0383
(801) 377-1288

Using the Q-DOS II Main Menu

Q-DOS II makes some standard DOS features much easier to use, and it provides other features not even available in DOS. Figure 5.1 shows the main menu of Q-DOS II. The top line of the screen displays a horizontal menu of primary options, from the standard directory-manipulation option to the option to print a file. A scrollable window of the files in the current directory also appears. A list of powerful function-key options is displayed at the left of the screen.

As you can see from the main menu line at the top of the screen, many Q-DOS II options are simply standard DOS commands. The difference lies in the convenience provided by the Q-DOS menu interface. For example, instead of having to specify a complete COPY command, entering file and path names, you use a more visual technique. You *tag*, or graphically select, the directories and files you want copied and their destinations. You can easily see directories by moving along the directory tree (see Figure 5.2) and pressing ↵, which displays a sorted list of files that reside in the selected directory.

```
Directory  Tag  View  Copy  Move  Find  Erase  Rename  Space  Attribute  Print
Change current directory, make or remove directory, see directory tree

 PATH   >> C:\

Count          Total Size    | File Name     | Size         | Date     | Time
                             | AUTOEXEC.BAK  |         430  |  8- 3-89 |  3:55p
 12  Files      112,318      | AUTOEXEC.BAT  |         417  |  8- 7-89 | 10:22a
                             | CAD           | <DIRECTORY>  |  1- 1-80 | 12:00a
  8  Directories             | COMMAND  .COM |      25,307  |  3-17-87 | 12:00p
                             | CONFIG   .SYS |         160  |  4- 5-88 |  6:00p
  0  Tagged           0      | DBASE         | <DIRECTORY>  |  1- 1-80 | 12:00a
                             | DOS           | <DIRECTORY>  |  1- 1-80 | 12:00a
F1- Help        F2- Status   | FRECOVER.DAT  |      28,672  |  8- 7-89 | 10:22a
F3- Chg Drive   F4- Prev Dir | IBMBIO   .COM |      22,100  |  3-18-87 | 12:00p
F5- Chg Dir     F6- DOS Cmd  | IBMDOS   .COM |      30,159  |  3-17-87 | 12:00p
F7- Srch Spec   F8- Sort     | IMCAPS        | <DIRECTORY>  |  1- 1-80 | 12:11a
F9- Edit       F10- Quit     | LOTUS         | <DIRECTORY>  |  1- 1-80 | 12:00a
  SPACE BAR- Tag file        | PREMENU$.BAT  |         128  |  6- 1-89 | 12:33p
  ESC- Abort Command         | QD2      .LOG |       3,206  |  1- 1-80 | 12:11a
                             | SAFEPARK.EXE  |       1,244  | 11-12-87 |  3:11p
Q-DOS II -- Version 2.00     | TREEINFO.NCD  |         443  |  5-28-88 |  6:33p
   Copyright (c) 1986        | UTILITY       | <DIRECTORY>  |  1- 1-80 | 12:00a
GAZELLE SYSTEMS - Provo, Utah
```

Figure 5.1: Q-DOS II main menu

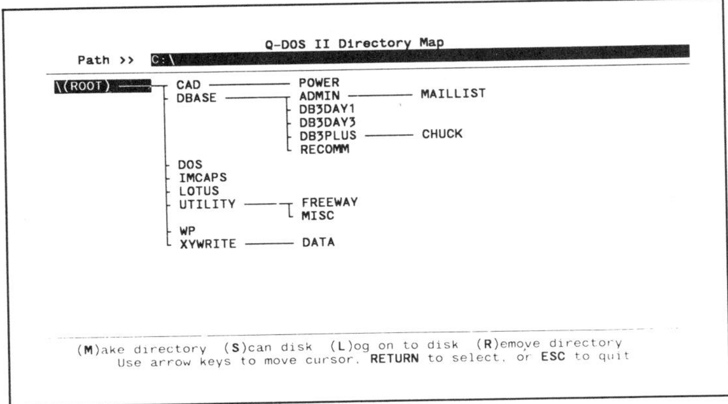

Figure 5.2: Visual tree of the disk's directory structure

Using a menu of choices at the bottom of the screen, you can create (M) or delete (R) directories, scan other disks to assess their directory structure (S), and set Q-DOS II's default drive (L).

The Function Keys Function key F1 offers the standard textual help screens explaining Q-DOS II's features. This capability has become almost obligatory in software packages nowadays. As implemented here, it offers an indexed list of choosable Q-DOS II features. Separate explanatory screens are displayed according to your menu choice.

Pressing F2 brings up a system status screen which contains a series of both DOS and Q-DOS II settings. Current system date and time are displayed, as well as installed and free memory. The boot drive is indicated, and all recognized physical and logical drive identifiers are displayed. As for Q-DOS II, the files selected for display (the display filter requirements) are shown, as well as the current sorting sequence. Especially for keyboards without keycap lights, this display also indicates the status of the Caps Lock, Num Lock, and Scroll Lock keys.

Function key F3 enables you to change the current Q-DOS II default drive. In conjunction with F4, which allows you to switch between the current and the previous directory, you can manipulate files in different directories on two different drives. F5 also adds to the function key power, enabling you to swiftly select and display the file contents of any directory being displayed; using F5 avoids even the minor effort of going through the main menu *Directory* selection method.

Pressing F6 displays a single DOS command prompt line. Any individual DOS command can be entered at this time; or you can run a secondary command processor by pressing F8.

Use F7 to limit Q-DOS II's search criteria whenever you wish to operate on groups of files that can be described by a wildcard specification. This reduces your work in later tagging the files; you have fewer files of other types in your way in the file window display.

You can sort directory entries by name, extension, size, or date by pressing the F8 key, then selecting the order in which you want your file displays to appear. Although you see the files sorted in the Q-DOS II directory window, they will not be physically rearranged on the disk.

Pressing F9 will automatically call up the configured word processor or editing program. The currently highlighted file in Q-DOS II's window will be transmitted to the editing program for initial processing. A built-in editor is included with Q-DOS II, but you can reconfigure the program to automatically link to your own word processor.

F10 is self explanatory, giving you the option to leave Q-DOS II and return to the DOS command prompt. In the case of DOS 4, you will be returned to wherever you were when Q-DOS II was invoked.

View Some operations are performed on individual files, such as the *View* choice. As Figure 5.3 suggests, its advantage over a simple DOS TYPE statement is that any file can be viewed in either ASCII text form (N) or a combination hexadecimal form (H) similar to the one used by the Norton Utilities NU program.

Also available in the viewing capability is a filtering feature. Pressing F on your keyboard once turns on the ability to suppress the display of any ASCII codes above 127. Pressing F once more turns on the special 8th-bit filtering capability, which makes files prepared with the WordStar word processing program easily viewable.

When both filtering methods are turned off (the default), you see the actual data contents of a file, with each ASCII character shown in its standard form, regardless of whether it is a letter, number, punctuation, or special character (ASCII code above 127).

Tagging Files for Group Operations Most operations in Q-DOS II can be performed on individual or on groups of files. For example, in Figure 5.4, **C:\WP** has been entered as the path, and a series of files in this directory have been tagged or marked simply by pressing the Space bar when the filename is highlighted. Notice that the windows to the left indicate that, even though they are not all visible, the directory contains 35 files (480K) of which 21 (147K) have been tagged for some upcoming operation.

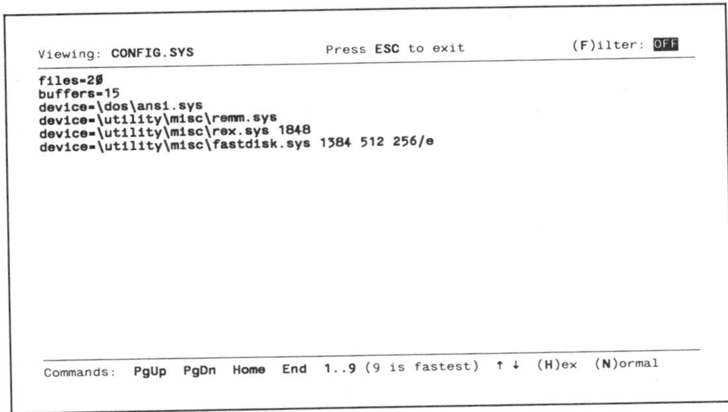

Figure 5.3: Viewing files with Q-DOS II

```
Directory  Tag  View  Copy  Move  Find  Erase  Rename  Space  Attribute  Print
Change current directory, make or remove directory, see directory tree

   PATH   >> C:\WP

 Count          Total Size      File Name         Size        Date       Time

 35   Files       480,668       NEWCHP19.WSD     27,392     5-28-88    11:00a
                                NEWCHP20.WSD     27,392     5-28-88     5:44p
  0   Directories              ▸ONEDAYS  .WP      4,608     4-30-86     4:33p
                                PALANTIR.WPO     81,536     1- 1-80     1:44a
 21   Tagged      147,068      ▸PDOUTLIN.WP       4,079    11- 5-87     3:11p
                                RESUME   .TXT     5,340    10-29-87     9:44a
                               ▸RESUME   .WP      5,248     7-17-89     6:22p
 F1- Help        F2- Status     RESUME   .WPB     5,248     7-17-89     6:22p
 F3- Chg Drive   F4- Prev Dir  ▸SHORTS   .WP      4,608    10- 4-85     3:33p
 F5- Chg Dir     F6- DOS Cmd   ▸SPEAKBK  .WP     26,347     9-14-87     3:44p
 F7- Srch Spec   F8- Sort       STANDARD.WPF        256     2- 1-84     8:11p
 F9- Edit        F10- Quit      STUFF    .DBF    35,968    12-13-87    10:00p
   SPACE BAR- Tag file         ▸SWITCH   .WP      1,230    10-29-87     8:55p
   ESC- Abort Command           WORK     .BLK       640    12- 2-87     2:33p
                                WP       .COM    21,760     7- 1-84    11:22a
 Q-DOS II -- Version 2.00       WPINSTAL.EXE     30,196     3-26-84     2:55p
     Copyright (c) 1986        ▸WRITEBK  .WP     24,078     9-14-87     2:11p
 GAZELLE SYSTEMS - Provo, Utah
```

Figure 5.4: Tagging files in a directory

They could all be operated on now as a group by simply selecting the operation desired from the main menu at the top of the screen. The following main-menu commands can operate on a group of files, treating each one in the group successively and automatically: Tag, Copy, Move, Erase, Rename, Attribute, and Print. Each of these choices leads to an appropriate following display, on which you can further specify the operation. For instance, selecting **Move** after tagging files in the C:\WP directory in Figure 5.4 would produce the screen shown in Figure 5.5. The directory tree is displayed automatically, along with the path to the *Moving from*: directory, entered at the previous stage. You are now expected to use your cursor keys to highlight the desired destination directory. As you move the highlighting cursor around the directory tree, Q-DOS II adjusts the entry in the *Moving to*: field. The user has highlighted the DATA subdirectory, and its full path is now shown on the *To*: line. Once ↵ is pressed, all the tagged files will be moved.

Print Whether or not you've previously tagged a set of files, selecting Print typically produces the submenu choices seen in Figure 5.6. Either the single file under the cursor can be printed (the same alternative is given for other operations such as Move or Copy), or all files previously tagged can be printed.

The Print menu offers a Map option, to print a graphic tree image of the disk's directory structure, and a Dir listing, which simply prints

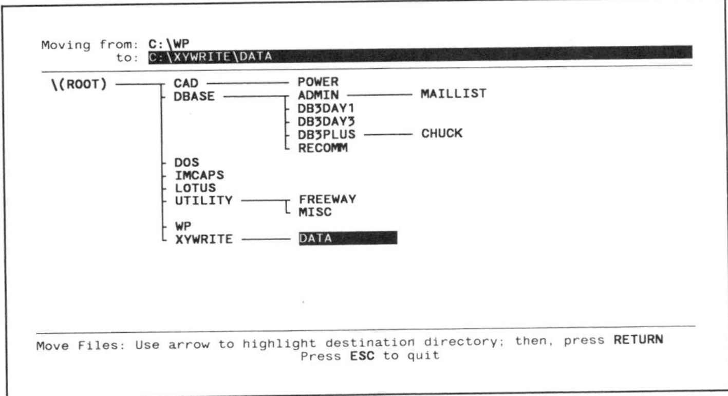

Figure 5.5: Moving files between directories

```
Print files:   Highlighted  Tagged  Map  Dir listing
Print the highlighted file

PATH  >> C:\

Count            Total Size    File Name        Size          Date       Time
12  Files          112,318     AUTOEXEC.BAK            430    8- 3-89    3:55p
 8  Directories                AUTOEXEC.BAT            417    8- 7-89   10:22a
 0  Tagged               0     CAD             <DIRECTORY>    1- 1-80   12:00a
                               COMMAND  .COM        25,307    3-17-87   12:00p
F1- Help       F2- Status      CONFIG   .SYS           160    4- 5-88    6:00p
F3- Chg Drive  F4- Prev Dir    DBASE           <DIRECTORY>    1- 1-80   12:00a
F5- Chg Dir    F6- DOS Cmd     DOS             <DIRECTORY>    1- 1-80   12:00a
F7- Srch Spec  F8- Sort        FRECOVER.DAT         28,672    8- 7-89   10:22a
F9- Edit       F10- Quit       IBMBIO   .COM        22,100    3-18-87   12:00p
 SPACE BAR- Tag file           IBMDOS   .COM        30,159    3-17-87   12:00p
 ESC- Abort Command            IMCAPS          <DIRECTORY>    1- 1-80   12:11a
                               LOTUS           <DIRECTORY>    1- 1-80   12:00a
Q-DOS II -- Version 2.00       PREMENU$.BAT            128    6- 1-89   12:33p
  Copyright (c) 1986           QD2      .LOG         3,206    8- 7-89   10:33a
GAZELLE SYSTEMS - Provo, Utah  SAFEPARK.EXE          1,244   11-12-87    3:11p
                               TREEINFO.NCD            443    5-28-88    6:33p
                               UTILITY         <DIRECTORY>    1- 1-80   12:00a
```

Figure 5.6: Submenu choices on the Print command

out the entries in the directory (files and directories), and their sizes and date/time values.

Attribute The Attribute command can be used to display all attribute values of the files in a directory, as shown in Figure 5.7, or it can be used to actually change the attribute values of individual files, as shown in Figure 5.8.

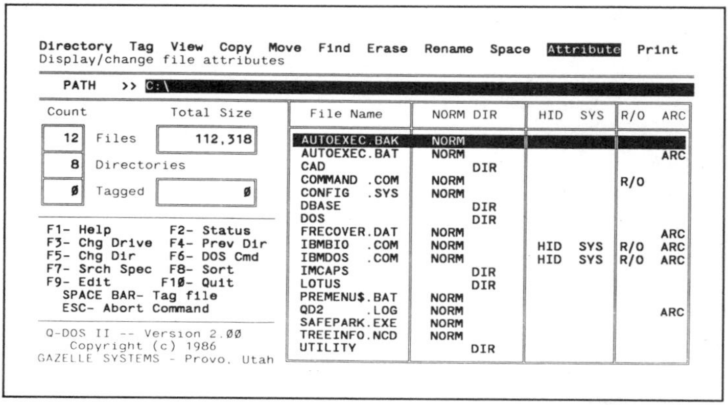

```
Directory  Tag  View  Copy  Move  Find  Erase  Rename  Space  Attribute  Print
Display/change file attributes
  PATH    >> C:\
 Count            Total Size     | File Name     | NORM DIR | HID  SYS | R/O  ARC
                                 | AUTOEXEC.BAK  | NORM     |          |
 [ 12] Files     [   112,318]    | AUTOEXEC.BAT  | NORM     |          |      ARC
 [  8] Directories               | CAD           |      DIR |          |
 [  0] Tagged    [         0]    | COMMAND  .COM | NORM     |          | R/O
                                 | CONFIG   .SYS | NORM     |          |
                                 | DBASE         |      DIR |          |
 F1- Help          F2- Status    | DOS           |      DIR |          |
 F3- Chg Drive     F4- Prev Dir  | FRECOVER.DAT  | NORM     |          |      ARC
 F5- Chg Dir       F6- DOS Cmd   | IBMBIO   .COM | NORM     | HID  SYS | R/O  ARC
 F7- Srch Spec     F8- Sort      | IBMDOS   .COM | NORM     | HID  SYS | R/O  ARC
 F9- Edit         F10- Quit      | IMCAPS        |      DIR |          |
   SPACE BAR- Tag file           | LOTUS         |      DIR |          |
   ESC- Abort Command            | PREMENU$.BAT  | NORM     |          |
                                 | QD2      .LOG | NORM     |          |      ARC
 Q-DOS II -- Version 2.00        | SAFEPARK.EXE  | NORM     |          |
    Copyright (c) 1986           | TREEINFO.NCD  | NORM     |          |
 GAZELLE SYSTEMS - Provo, Utah   | UTILITY       |      DIR |          |
```

Figure 5.7: Directory listing of file attributes

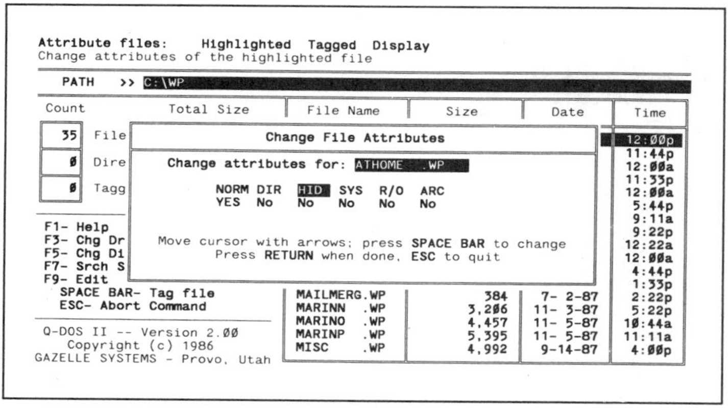

```
Attribute files:    Highlighted  Tagged  Display
Change attributes of the highlighted file
  PATH    >> C:\WP
 Count        Total Size   | File Name      |      Size |    Date  |  Time
 [ 35] File  +-----------------------------------------------+  12:00p
 [  0] Dire  |           Change File Attributes              |  11:44p
 [  0] Tagg  |                                               |  12:00a
             | Change attributes for: ATHOME   .WP           |  11:33p
 F1- Help    |                                               |  12:00a
 F3- Chg Dr  |      NORM DIR  HID  SYS  R/O  ARC             |   5:44p
 F5- Chg Di  |      YES  No   No   No   No   No              |   9:11a
 F7- Srch S  |                                               |   9:22p
 F9- Edit    | Move cursor with arrows; press SPACE BAR to change | 12:22a
             |     Press RETURN when done, ESC to quit       |  12:00a
             +-----------------------------------------------+   4:44p
                                                                 1:33p
   SPACE BAR- Tag file     | MAILMERG.WP    |       384 |  7- 2-87 |  2:22p
   ESC- Abort Command      | MARINN   .WP   |     3,206 | 11- 3-87 |  5:22p
                           | MARINO   .WP   |     4,457 | 11- 5-87 | 10:44a
 Q-DOS II -- Version 2.00  | MARINP   .WP   |     5,395 | 11- 5-87 | 11:11a
    Copyright (c) 1986     | MISC     .WP   |     4,992 |  9-14-87 |  4:00p
 GAZELLE SYSTEMS - Provo, Utah
```

Figure 5.8: Changing the attributes of an individual file

Space and Find You will often use the Space and Find commands. Keeping track of how much space on your disk is in use and how much is available is part of the job performed by the DOS CHKDSK command. However, CHKDSK is slower than Q-DOS II, in part because it does more than simple space identification. Figure 5.9 displays the result of asking Q-DOS II to check on the space for drive C.

The Find command is used to locate a file. You may know that a particular file exists somewhere on a disk but not be sure which directory it is in. Q-DOS II's Find command shown in Figure 5.10, very rapidly tracks down all instances of the file (s).

This feature is also particularly useful when you have multiple copies of a file, and you want to locate them all to determine which is the most recent version. As Figure 5.10 also suggests, you can use this method to determine how many independent copies of COMMAND.COM exist

```
Directory  Tag  View  Copy  Move  Find  Erase  Rename  Space  Attribute  Print
Show the total, used, and free space on any disk

 PATH   >> C:\WP

Count          Total Size    File Name          Size        Date       Time

 35  Files        480,668    ATHOME   .WP       4,949     11- 5-87   12:00p
                             AUCLIST  .WP      16,000     11-10-87   11:44p
  0  Directories             AUCTION  .WP       2,432     10-29-86   12:00a
                             BOOKTOC  .TXT      7,120     12-28-87   11:33p
  0  Tagged             0    DEFAULT  .WP         256      4- 5-86   12:00a
                                                                          p
                           Space On Disk C                                a
F1- Help        F2-                                                       p
F3- Chg Drive   F4-                                                       a
F5- Chg Dir     F6-      Total space:         10,584,064                  a
F7- Srch Spec   F8-                                                       p
F9- Edit        F10-     Total used:           7,798,784                  p
  SPACE BAR- Tag f                                                        p
  ESC- Abort Comma       Total available:      2,785,280                  p
                                                                          a
Q-DOS II -- Versio         Press any key to continue                      a
   Copyright (c) 1                                                        p
GAZELLE SYSTEMS - Provo, Utah
```

Figure 5.9: Checking available disk space

```
Directory  Tag  View  Copy  Move  Find  Erase  Rename  Space  Attribute  Print
Search all directories on the disk to find specified file(s)

 PATH   >> C:\WP

Count          Total Size    File Name          Size        Date       Time

 35  File                  Find File                                 12:00p
                                                                     11:44p
  0  Dire                                                            12:00a
           Enter the file name to find:  COMMAND.COM                 11:33p
  0  Tagg                                                            12:00a
                                                                      5:44p
           Enter a file name, or a 'wildcard' specification           9:11a
F1- Help     using the global '*' and/or '?' characters               9:22p
F3- Chg Dr                                                           12:22a
F5- Chg Di    Press CTRL-R to recall the last find pattern           12:00a
F7- Srch S                                                            4:44p
F9- Edit                                                              1:33p
  SPACE BAR- Tag file        MAILMERG.WP          384      7- 2-87    2:22p
  ESC- Abort Command         MARINN   .WP       3,206     11- 3-87    5:22p
                             MARINO   .WP       4,457     11- 5-87   10:44a
Q-DOS II -- Version 2.00     MARINP   .WP       5,395     11- 5-87   11:11a
   Copyright (c) 1986        MISC     .WP       4,992      9-14-87    4:00p
GAZELLE SYSTEMS - Provo, Utah
```

Figure 5.10: Finding files within a hard-disk tree structure

on your disk, each potentially needing to be upgraded for your latest revision of your DOS software.

Overall, these examples don't actually do justice to the sense of control of your hard disk, its directory structure, and the most common DOS operations and commands that Q-DOS II gives you. The enhanced aspects, such as file moving and improved file viewing, make this an invaluable addition to your DOS system. It is a dramatic improvement over DOS versions 3.31 and earlier. Even for those of you who decide to upgrade to DOS 4, Q-DOS II still remains a viable alternative hard-disk interface program.

Overall, DOS 4 offers the bulk of features available in the current version of Q-DOS II. Some of the utility package aspects remain superior, such as being able to tag and print multiple files, or being able to easily call up your own editor at will for any tagged file. However, a major factor to consider at this point is still the fact that Q-DOS II can be used to offer all these management features for nearly any version of DOS. You needn't upgrade to DOS 4. If you deal with many machines, each of which may be on a different version of DOS, then using Q-DOS II affords you its range of features on all your systems.

Tips on Using Q-DOS II

- Use the Q-DOS II configuration program to change the name and location of the built-in editor to the appropriate name and location of your own word processing program. Pressing F9 then will bring up your program (assuming you have enough memory) with the text file currently being highlighted on the Q-DOS II screen display.
- One of the reasons Q-DOS II is so fast is that it relies on a log file placed in the root directory of each disk. This log file (QD2.LOG) contains a specially formatted set of entries that specify the directory tree structure of your disk. Using this log file assumes that you have made no directory adjustments outside of Q-DOS II. If you use commands outside of Q-DOS II to restructure your disk, you will have to Scan (S command on the Directory map display) the disk again to recreate the log file.

This file saves Q-DOS II the time necessary to scan and establish the entire disk's tree structure each time you bring up the program, as well as each time you switch to a new hard disk on a multi-drive system.

CHAPTER 6

Making Backup Copies with Back-It

Making backup copies can sometimes be very complicated, especially if you don't want or need to back up an entire disk. The process can take a long time and invites making simple mistakes, such as inserting the wrong diskette or forgetting a group of files. DOS provides the BACKUP and RESTORE commands for backing up and restoring files on your hard disk, but these commands can be cumbersome, inflexible, and slow. One alternative is a sophisticated backup utility program called Back-It. This program has some significant benefits for hard-disk users:

- Back-It writes data to backup diskettes significantly faster than DOS's BACKUP command. Back-It uses an advanced Direct Memory Access (DMA) technique for writing to floppies. In addition to faster I/O methods for writing to an individual floppy drive, Back-It can use multiple floppy drives during backup operations to increase the overall throughput even further.
- Back-It uses sophisticated error-prevention and correction techniques to minimize potential problems with unreliable diskettes. Bad sectors on diskettes used for backup are locked out so that your files are not written onto these bad sectors. Data unwittingly written onto existing bad sectors could be very difficult to read from later. Back-It also includes automatic corrective techniques for enhancing its ability to read backup data from diskettes that have become damaged after a backup.

- Back-It offers much greater flexibility than the DOS commands BACKUP and RESTORE. You can conveniently select any or all directories within the tree structure for backup and include or exclude any combination of filenames using multiple wildcard expressions. You can also restore any or all files from a set of backup diskettes.
- Back-It provides built-in capabilities to format diskettes for different storage sizes, and can automatically format diskettes even during the backup process. Back-It does not require diskettes to be preformatted, as does the DOS command BACKUP.
- The full-screen graphic interface of Back-It is easier to use than is DOS's traditionally difficult command line. Even DOS 4 still requires you to understand and specify a complex string of parameters and switches. Back-It offers a more visual graphic menu and window interface for specifying the equivalent of input parameters and command switch settings.
- Back-It provides on-line statistics on your screen, showing how many files have been selected by your specifications, how many bytes they consume, how many diskettes will be taken up by the overall backup, and how far along the backup process is.
- Back-It includes a List feature, which enables you to display, print, or even save to a file a listing of all files stored on a backup diskette. The source directories of these files are also indicated at the same time.

Back-It is available from:

Gazelle Systems
42 North University Avenue, Suite 10
Provo, Utah 84601
(800) 233-0383
(801) 377-1288

Using the Back-It Main Menu

Back-It's main menu, shown at the top of the screen in Figure 6.1, presents a familiar horizontal menu approach to functions and features. After moving the highlight cursor to select any option, you can press ⟵ to initiate the highlighted option. As is common in this type of layout, the second line offers a succinct phrase explaining what the option will do if it is selected. In fact, the lowermost window on the screen always displays a more detailed paragraph of information about the currently highlighted menu option (unless you turn off the help display).

As you can see in Figure 6.1, the screen is split into several smaller windows. Each window has an informational role to play. The thin topmost window shows the source and destination drives. In this example, files from drive C will be backed up on floppies in drive A. You can change either of these drive specifications by selecting *From-drive* or *To-drive* from the main menu.

The File Selection Parameters window is located just below the source/destination window. It reflects your file and directory choices to be backed up, as well as offering control over file date ranges. This window merely reflects current selections you have made, or defaults assigned by Back-It. The Select entry indicates whether all files (the default) or only modified files are to be backed up. After selecting *Modified* on the main menu, you receive a two-choice submenu and can explicitly tell Back-It whether to back up all files (in the directories chosen), or only to back up files which have been newly created or recently modified since the last backup operation of Back-It.

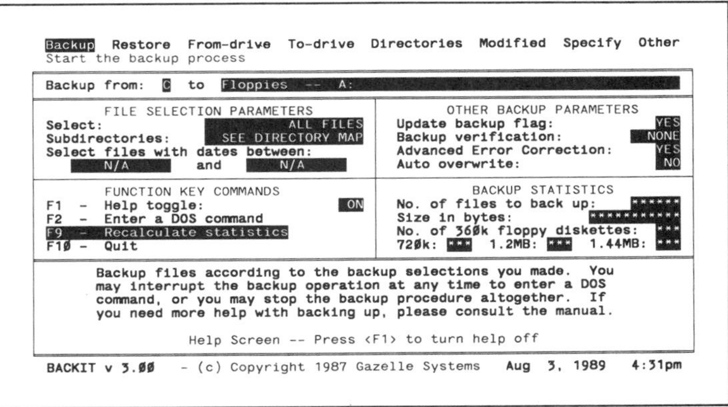

Figure 6.1: Back-It's main menu

As you'll see below, the Other submenu choice provides a number of additional possibilities. One of those options is to specify starting and ending dates for files to be included in the backup procedure.

Selecting Directories on the main menu calls up the screen shown in Figure 6.2. The Figure shows a graphic tree of all the directories on the C drive, with the directories selected for inclusion in the backup marked by a solid right-pointing arrow.

In Figure 6.2, you use your cursor control keys to highlight individual directory names, then press the spacebar to tag each desired directory for backup purposes. When you have completed tagging each directory you want to back up, you press the Return key to return to the Back-It main menu. At this point, you can either select *Backup* from the main menu to begin backup processing, or you can take other preparatory steps.

As you can see, it's quite easy to select individual and unrelated directories from your directory tree for backing up. It is also easy to select individual files from those directories to be written to the backup diskettes. Figure 6.3 presents the pop-up window that results from selecting *Specify* from the main Back-It menu. You can enter up to ten separate specifications of filenames to include in the backup. You can also enter another ten filename specifications to exclude.

These inclusion and exclusion specifications can use wildcards, as shown in Figure 6.3, but they need not rely on wildcards. In this

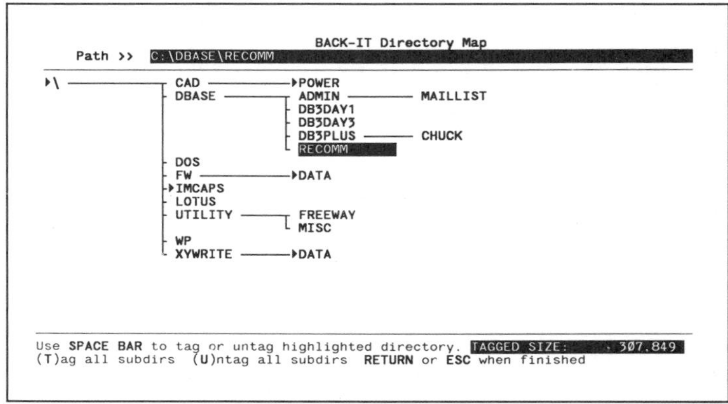

Figure 6.2: Back-It's Directory Map

example, all .EXE and .COM files are excluded from backup, because they are presumed to be unchanging executable files that probably exist on original diskettes elsewhere. If you had a large client database, called CLIENTS.DBF, that you wanted to back up regularly, you could replace the *.* specification in the INCLUDE column shown in Figure 6.3 with CLIENTS.DBF. Then you could select the correct directory from the *Directories* menu. Lastly, you could store this unique configuration by choosing *Other* from the main menu to obtain the screen shown in Figure 6.4.

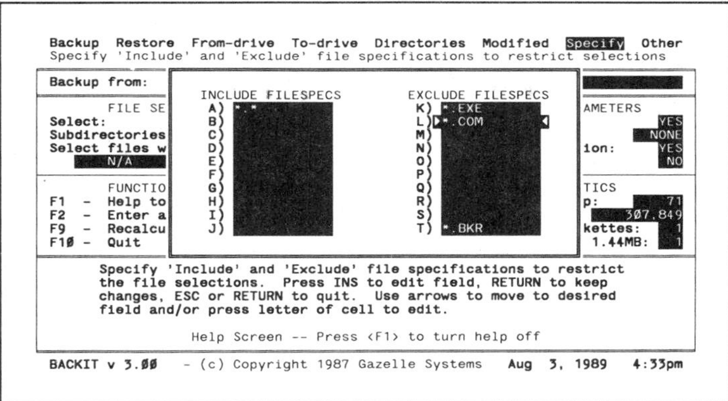

Figure 6.3: Back-It's Specify screen

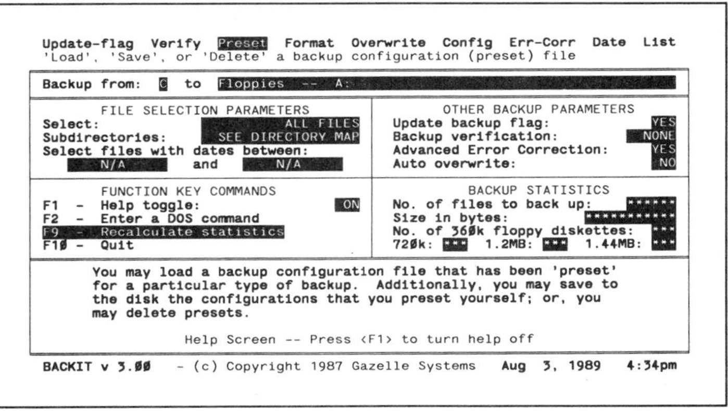

Figure 6.4: The Other menu choices

Figure 6.4 represents a miscellaneous set of other options, functions, and features available in Back-It. These nine choices represent a submenu obtained when you select *Other* from the main menu. Selecting one of these nine submenu choices will either produce a direct request for data entry or display another level of menu choices. As is common with horizontal menus, the line below the menu itself is used as a one-line message explaining what a particular menu choice will do. Here, you can see that actually selecting *Preset* will display another submenu with three choices—saving the current configuration of selections and responses, loading into memory a previously saved configuration, or deleting from disk a previously saved configuration.

Saving the configuration in a settings file means storing on disk all existing menu choices, along with option entries such as directories selected, inclusion/exclusion specifications, and so forth. You can then reset all values later by merely loading the desired file of preset values. You can have an unlimited number of configurations stored in separate Back-It configuration files. You can load a file of presets at any time either by using this Preset choice or by specifying the Preset filename as the first parameter when you invoke Back-It itself from DOS.

One of the many other useful features available from this Other menu is the *List* choice. If you invoke this option as you're defining the scope of a backup operation, you can later list all files on your backup diskette(s). The listing can be sent to the screen, to your printer, or to a disk file for later manipulation by your word processor.

The three other windows on a Back-It screen offer both controls and information.

Other Backup Parameters The Other Backup Parameters window, seen in the upper-right portion of the screen, reflects the results of four key parameter values set through main-menu and submenu choices. All four of these indicators can be set or reset through direct choices on the *Other* submenu (see Figure 6.4). These include 1) whether the file backup flags are reset after the file is successfully backed up to diskette, 2) the type of file verification used during the writing operations, 3) the type of error-correction logic used to ensure valid file copies, and 4) whether diskettes are to be automatically written to, even if there is pre-existing data on the diskette.

The Function Keys in Back-It The Function Key Commands window shows only the four function keys used in Back-It; these keys are always active and available when the program is running. Pressing any one of them performs an immediate function. The currently highlighted menu or submenu choices are not affected or changed. Only the requested function key chore is performed.

As in many programs, F1 serves as a Help key though its role is somewhat modified here. Because the bottom window of each screen normally contains help information, pressing F1 acts only as a toggle to suppress the display of this help text. F10 also plays a familiar role, enabling you to exit to DOS while Back-It is running.

F2 offers a convenient opportunity to enter a standard DOS command from within Back-It. If you have sufficient memory, you can even run another program. F9 can be pressed at any time to recalculate the information seen in the Backup Statistics window. The asterisks seen initially are replaced by the actual numbers determined by your earlier selections, such as those entered in Figures 6.2 and 6.3.

Pressing F9 results in the sample new screen shown in Figure 6.5. Given the exclusions and the selected directories, 70 files totalling 264,123 bytes will be written out to the backup drive. In this case, only one diskette is needed, no matter what the density of your diskette drive is.

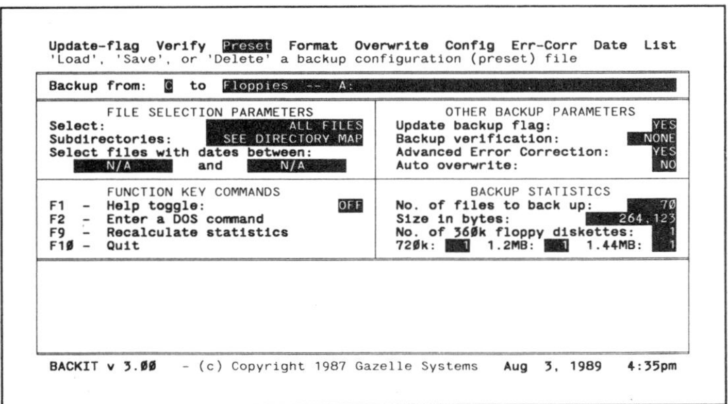

Figure 6.5: Backup Statistics display

The Backup Process At this point, you've completed all your preparatory steps. You've specified which directories are to be included, which files are to be selected, and what constraints are to be considered. You've saved the configuration for future use, and you've used F9 to determine how many diskettes will be needed.

The actual backup process does not formally begin until you select *Backup* from the main menu, as seen in Figure 6.6. At this time, the Help window is replaced by a progress report window.

During the backup process, you will be constantly informed how far along the backup has progressed and which files are actually being written. Figure 6.7 demonstrates the progress report during the middle of this example single diskette backup. Filenames and statistical percentages are shown in the Help window, while read/write/track information is shown in a pop-up window in the center of the screen.

One final but important note about the backup capabilities of this product. Although the Backup Parameters window is partly obscured in Figure 6.8, you can see that when you back up a large number of files, many diskettes will be needed. Over 7Mb of data can require twenty three 360K diskettes, or even six 1.44Mb floppies. Back-It has the ability to initiate and manage writing to multiple disk drives (up to four). This can make your backup even faster, and it offers an additional advantage for those of you with extra diskette drives on your system. Remember that an additional advantage

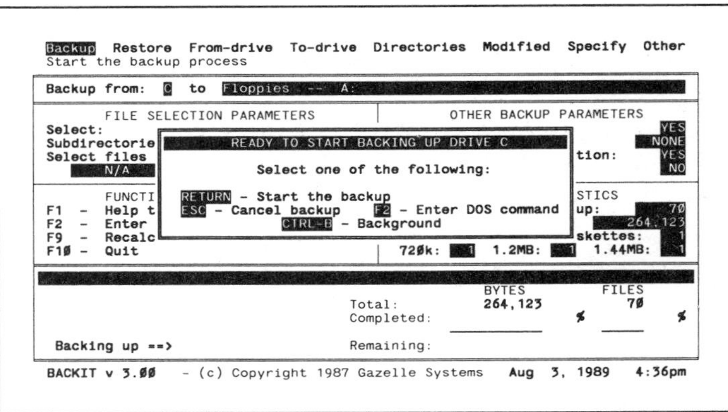

Figure 6.6: Beginning the actual* Backup *process

of Back-It over DOS's BACKUP command is the automatic diskette formatting when necessary. DOS requires that the FORMAT command be accessible when necessary, and if you are using DOS 3.X, you must have specified the /F switch before initiating the BACKUP. Since Back-It incorporates a formatting algorithm within itself, it can quickly and automatically begin formatting a diskette when necessary.

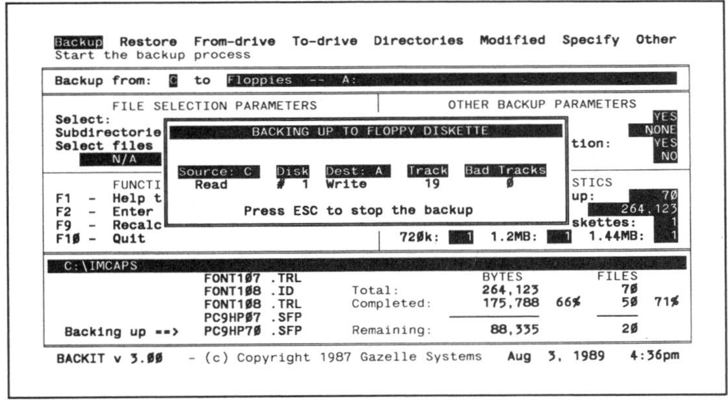

Figure 6.7: Backup in progress

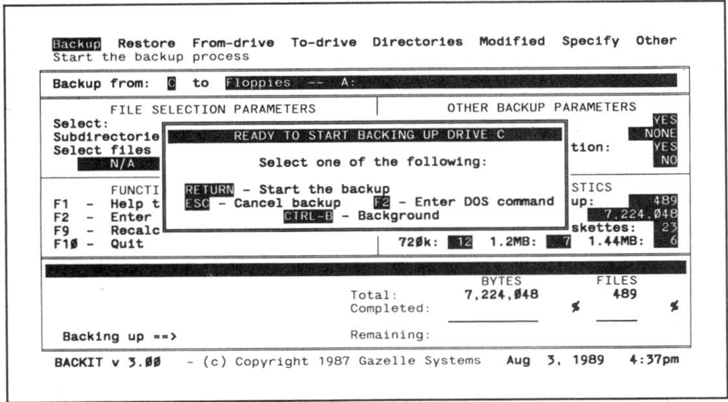

Figure 6.8: Backup Statistics for a large group of files

Restorations Most of the time, you back up your files for protection, never needing to actually use those backup diskettes to restore information. However, there may come a time when you accidentally delete a critical file, or a sector goes bad on your disk and an important file just happens to be using that sector. Then, you'll need to reverse the backup process. If you used the DOS BACKUP command, you'll need to use the DOS RESTORE command. However, if you used Back-It, you need only bring it up once again on your screen and select the Restore main-menu choice.

Restoration is another area where Back-It shines over its DOS counterpart, the RESTORE command. With Back-It, you can more fully specify which directories and which file sets are to be restored. This means that only one Back-It run can restore all desired files, no matter how diversely situated or named they are. In addition, you can individually restore or skip over files during the restoration process. This design means that restoration under Back-It is significantly easier and faster than under the DOS BACKUP command.

Placing the first of your backup diskettes into drive A and then pressing ↵ begins the restoration process seen in progress in Figure 6.9. As Figure 6.9 suggests, Back-It displays statistics as it scans your backup diskettes and restores some or all of the files found to your hard disk. It also displays a message window on your screen if it encounters difficulties reading any data sectors on your disk. When

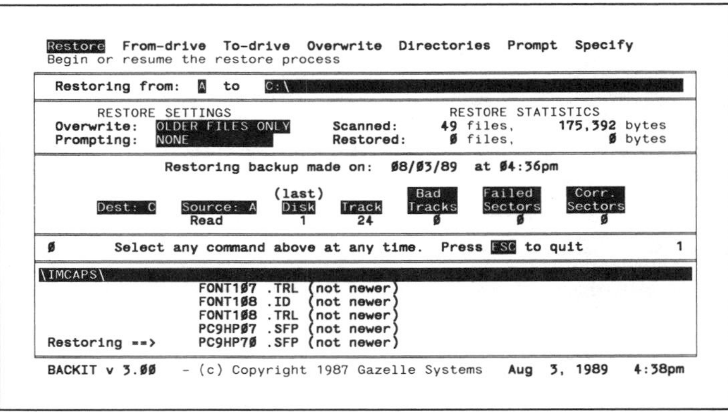

Figure 6.9: The Restore feature of Back-It

this occurs, it switches automatically into its advanced error correction logic mode, and recovers as much as possible from the problem sectors. Where another restoration process may fail completely, Back-It continues successfully, losing only the absolute minimum amount of irretrievable disk information. This feature alone makes the product worth using over DOS's BACKUP and RESTORE tandem commands.

Main-menu selections can be used to specify which files are to be restored, whether prompting is to take place, and whether files are to be updated based solely on name or whether date/time of creation is to be considered as well. In this example, the Overwrite setting is currently for "Older Files Only." This setting is visible on the screen, as is a parenthetical "not newer" expression for each file that is read from the backup floppy but not written onto the hard disk. This setting avoids accidentally overwriting a newer file on your hard disk with an older file from your backup diskette.

Tips on Using Back-It

- If you are careful to use diskettes containing no important information, you can speed up the backup process by selecting Auto-Overwrite. This enables Back-It to skip the protective pause during which you are informed that the diskette to be used for backup contains existing files.
- Use the Preset capability to avoid having to reestablish a complex group of backup settings. Create multiple Preset files if you have multiple backup groups, invoking Back-It with a different Preset file each time.
- Use the include/exclude file specification feature (*Specify* menu choice) as well as the *Directories* menu choice to select only desired directories to back up.
- Backup your entire disk once, then perform only incremental backups. An incremental backup copies only files that are new or changed since the last backup. Flags are kept on the disk by DOS, but are maintained by Back-It for this incremental backup purpose.

Part III

Appendices

APPENDIX A

Glossary

This appendix defines all of the important terms you'll encounter in this book and in other discussions of hard disk management with any version of DOS through 4. This glossary offers concise definitions that can quickly refresh your memory when you are at your computer, or at any time that you simply can't remember the meaning of a particular term.

active partition The section of a hard disk containing the operating system to be used when the hardware powers up.

application software Programs whose purpose is to carry out some real-world operation that the user would otherwise have to perform manually. Word processors and spreadsheet packages are examples of application software. Systems software, by contrast, is designed to perform the internal, "housekeeping" operations that enable a computer to run application software.

archive bit A bit in a file specification that indicates whether the file in question needs to be backed up.

AUTOEXEC.BAT A batch file executed automatically whenever the computer is started. It usually includes commands to set the prompt and path, to set initial values for environmental variables, and to invoke appropriate memory-resident (TSR) programs.

base name The portion of a file name to the left of the period separator; it can be up to eight characters long. *See also* **file name, file-name extension**.

batch file An ASCII file containing a sequence of DOS commands that, when invoked, assume control of the computer, executing the commands as if they were entered successively by a computer user.

bit One-eighth of a byte. A bit is a binary digit, either 0 or 1. *See also* **byte**.

block device Any input/output peripheral that transfers data in groups of characters, called *blocks*. By contrast, *character* devices transfer data one byte at a time.

booting up *See* **bootstrapping**.

boot record The section on a disk that contains the minimum information DOS needs to start the system. The boot record contains the system ID, the number of bytes per sector, and the number of sectors per cluster. It also contains the number of system-reserved sectors, the number of FAT copies, the maximum number of root directory entries, and the total number of sectors on your hard disk. Last, it contains a format ID, the number of sectors per FAT and per track, and the number of disk heads.

bootstrapping The process by which a computer starts operating when it is first turned on or restarted with Ctrl-Alt-Del. DOS contains the instructions a computer needs to carry out its startup operations, and nearly all of DOS is stored on disk. The computer's ROM contains a small set of instructions—the bootstrap routine—the system needs to locate the DOS routines and thus "pull itself up by its bootstraps." Computer users also speak of *booting* a disk or program; this simply means loading a program into memory and starting it. *See also* **cold booting, warm booting**.

buffer An area in memory set aside to speed up the transfer of data, allowing blocks of data to be transferred at once. See also **look-ahead buffers**.

byte The main unit of memory in a computer. A byte is an eight-bit binary number. One character usually takes up one byte. *See also* **bit**.

cache A portion of memory reserved for the contents of recently referenced disk sectors. Facilitates faster reaccess of the same sectors.

cluster A group of contiguous sectors on a disk; the smallest unit of disk storage that DOS can manipulate.

cold booting The type of bootstrapping that occurs when the computer's power is first turned on and DOS starts the computer operating. Cold booting involves more extensive internal testing than warm booting, which occurs after the computer is reset with Ctrl-Alt-Del. *See also* **bootstrapping, warm booting**.

COMMAND.COM The command processor supplied with DOS.

command line The line on which a command is entered. This line contains the command and all of its associated parameters and switches. In spite of the name, it may actually consume more than one screen line, since it is terminated by a carriage return.

command processor The program that translates and acts on commands.

COMSPEC The environment variable that contains the path leading to the resident command processor.

concatenation The placing of two text files together in a series.

CONFIG.SYS An ASCII text file containing system-configuration commands. To use the commands discussed in Chapter 3, you must include them in a CONFIG.SYS file.

configuration An initial set of system values, such as the number of buffers DOS will use, the number of simultaneously open files DOS will allow, and the specific devices that the system will support.

console The combination of your system's monitor and keyboard.

contiguous sectors Physically adjacent disk sectors used by a file.

copy protection Mechanism contained in diskettes that inhibits diskette copying using conventional commands.

CPU (Central Processing Unit) The main chip that executes all individual computer instructions.

Ctrl-Z The end-of-file marker.

cursor The blinking line or highlighting box that indicates where the next keystroke will be displayed or what data the next control code entered will affect.

cylinder Two tracks at the same radius on different sides of a double-sided disk; may be extended to include multiple platters on a hard disk. For example, side 0, track 30; side 1, track 30; side 2, track 30; and side 3, track 30 form a cylinder.

data area The tracks on a disk that contain user data.

database A collection of data organized into various categories. For example, a phone book is a database.

database management system A program that allows the creation of specially organized files, as well as data entry, manipulation, removal, and reporting for those files.

data disk A diskette that has been formatted without the /S switch. The disk contains data, not system, files.

default value The standard value of a variable or system parameter.

delimiter A special character, such as a comma or space, used to separate values or data entries.

destination The targeted location for data, files, or other information generated or moved by a DOS command. *Compare with* **source**.

device Any internal or external peripheral hardware.

device driver A special program that must be loaded before a device can be used; the part of DOS that first intercepts an interrupt. Also known as an interrupt handler.

device name Logical name that DOS uses to refer to a device.

digital A representation of numeric values based on a collection of individual digits, such as 0's and 1's in the binary number system.

directory A grouping of files on a disk. These files are displayed together and may include references to other directories (subdirectories).

directory tree The treelike structure created when a root directory has several subdirectories, each subdirectory has subdirectories, and so on.

disk drive A hardware device that accesses the data stored on a disk.

diskette A flexible, removable oxide-coated disk used to store data. Also called a floppy disk. *Compare with* **hard disk.**

disk optimizer A program that rearranges the location of files stored on a disk to make the data in those files more quickly retrievable.

DOS (Disk Operating System) A disk manager and the program that allows computer-user interaction.

DOS environment A part of memory set aside to hold certain default values, such as COMSPEC, PATH, LASTDRIVE, and so on, needed by DOS commands or application programs.

DOS prompt The visual indication that DOS is waiting for a command or prompting you for input; usually C> or A>.

double-density diskette A diskette on which magnetic storage material is arranged twice as densely as on diskettes commonly in use in the early days of IBM PCs, allowing the storage of twice the earlier amount of data. Usually refers to a 360K, 5¼-inch diskette. *Compare with* **high-capacity diskette.**

drive identifier A single letter representing a disk drive; for example, drive A or drive B. In commands, usually requires a colon after it; for example, A:.

DRIVER.SYS A file containing a device driver for an extra external disk drive. Used in the CONFIG.SYS file.

end-of-file marker A Ctrl-Z code that marks the logical end of a file.

environment *See* **DOS environment.**

error level A code, set by programs as they conclude processing, that tells DOS whether an error occurred and, if so, the severity of that error.

expanded memory Additional memory beyond the 640K program limit. It does not fill a continuous range, like conventional or extended memory, but rather is mapped to a window of reserved memory (in the 640K to 1Mb area). The mapping (or address adjustment) is handled by a special software device driver that adheres to the current Expanded Memory Specification (EMS).

expansion cards Add-on circuit boards through which hardware can increase the power of the system, such as one that adds extra memory or a modem.

expansion slots Connectors inside the computer in which expansion cards are placed so that they tie in directly to the system.

extended DOS partition A hard-disk partition used to exceed the 32Mb, single-disk barrier; it can be divided into logical disk drives. *Compare with* **primary DOS partition**.

extended memory In IBM PC AT and compatible computers based on the Intel 80286 microprocessor chip, built-in RAM ranging from 1 to 16Mb. The /E switch to the VDISK.SYS device driver, when it is included in your CONFIG.SYS file, makes this space accessible to DOS in the form of a RAM disk. *Compare with* **expanded memory**. *See also* **memory, RAM, RAM disk**.

external buffer A device, connected to the computer and another device, that stores data until the device is ready to accept it.

external command To the user, each command in DOS or a high-level language, such as BASIC, is a single instruction. To the computer, however, a single command is actually a series of the much more detailed machine-language instructions it needs. In effect, each command is actually a small program or routine, stored as a file. In DOS, these command files are either loaded into the computer's active memory along with the rest of DOS when the computer is turned on or stored on disk until needed. External, or nonresident, commands are those that are stored on disk until needed. To use an external command, you must make sure it is accessible to DOS. That is, either the command file must be located in the current default directory, or you must define a path to the directory where it is located. *Compare with* **internal command**.

file A collection of bytes, representing a program or data, stored as a named group on a disk.

file-allocation table (FAT) A table of clusters stored on a disk that tells DOS whether a given cluster is good, bad, continued, or the end of a chain of clusters.

file-control block A data structure used by some older programs to keep track of files in memory.

file locking A way to prevent a network user from accessing a file that is already in use by another user.

file name The name of a file on a disk. Usually refers to the base name, but can include the extension as well.

file-name extension The one to three characters after the period following the base name in a file specification. Used to specify the type of information in a file.

filter A program that accepts data as input, processes it in some manner, and then outputs the data in a different form.

fixed disk IBM term for a hard disk.

floppy disk *See* **diskette**.

formatting Low-level formatting places timing marks on a disk to arrange the tracks and sectors for subsequent reading and writing;

such formatting normally is done by a disk manufacturer. High-level formatting, done by you with the DOS FORMAT command, creates a root directory, a boot record, and a file-allocation table.

fragmentation A condition in which many different files have been stored in noncontiguous clusters on a disk.

function keys Special-purpose keys on a keyboard, which can be assigned unique tasks by DOS or by application programs.

global characters *See* **wildcards**.

hard disk A device, consisting of one or more rigid platters and read/write heads, that stores data at a higher density than a floppy diskette and allows faster access. It is sealed in an airtight compartment to avoid contaminants that could damage or destroy the disk. *Compare with* **diskette**.

hardware The physical components of a computer system. *Compare with* **software**.

head crash A collision between the read/write head and the disk platter of a hard disk, which physically damages the disk and the data on it.

help file A file of textual information containing explanations of commands and modes along with other on-screen tutorial information.

hidden files Files whose names do not appear in a directory listing. Usually refer to DOS's internal system files, IBMBIO.COM (or IO.SYS) and IBMDOS.COM (or MSDOS.SYS), but can also refer to certain files used in copy-protection schemes.

high-capacity diskette A 1.2Mb, 5¼-inch floppy diskette. *Compare with* **double-density diskette**.

housekeeping For directories and files, making sure the directory stays intact and well organized and that unnecessary files are deleted. Broadly, any activity, by the user or the machine itself, directed toward maintaining the system rather than running application software to produce results.

hub The center hole of a diskette.

internal command To the user, each command in DOS or a high-level language such as BASIC is a single instruction. To the computer, however, a single command is actually a series of the much more detailed machine-language instructions it needs. In effect, each command is actually a small program or routine, stored as a file. In DOS, these command files are either loaded into the computer's active memory along with the rest of DOS when the computer is turned on or stored on disk until needed. Internal, or resident, commands are those that are loaded into memory along with the rest of DOS. *Compare with* **external command**.

I/O (input/output) Information accepted by the CPU (input) or sent by the CPU to a peripheral device (output).

kernel The part of DOS that performs high-level file management. Contained in the hidden file MSDOS.SYS on MS-DOS systems, or in IBMDOS.COM in PC-DOS systems.

key combination When two or more keys are pressed simultaneously, as in Ctrl-ScrollLock or Ctrl-Alt-Del.

key redefinition Assigning a nonstandard value to a key.

kilobyte (K) 1024 bytes.

line feed When the cursor on a screen moves to the next line, or when the print head on a printer moves down the paper to the next line. Caused by transmission of a control code (ASCII 10 or Ctrl-J) to the print or display device.

literal Data, such as a command parameter, that is accepted exactly as it was submitted and not interpreted as a control code.

lockup A state in which the computer will not accept any input and may have stopped processing. The computer must be rebooted to resume operation.

log file A separate file, created with the DOS command BACKUP, that keeps track of the names of all files written to the backup diskettes.

logical Defined based on a decision, not by physical properties; also, having a purely conceptual (virtual), rather than a physical, existence.

logical drives Disk drives, created in an extended DOS partition, that do not exist as separate physical disk drives, although DOS treats them as if they do. Not to be confused with virtual or RAM disks, which are created in memory rather than on disk.

look-ahead buffers 512-byte memory buffers used by DOS 4 to read successively positioned disk sectors before those sectors are actually referenced by a program or command, thereby improving performance. They are created by the BUFFERS command.

machine language The most fundamental format in which to program a computer, using instructions made up entirely of strings of 0's and 1's.

macro A set of commands, often memory resident, that are activated by a single command or keystroke. When executed, they appear to the program executing them as if they were being entered by the user.

megabyte (Mb) 1024 kilobytes.

memory The circuitry in a computer that stores information. *See also* **RAM**.

memory resident Available in physical memory for immediate execution, as opposed to being loaded from a disk file.

menu A set of choices displayed in tabular format.

microfloppy diskette A 3½-inch diskette format used in the new IBM Personal System/2 and many other computers.

multitasking Two or more computing applications executing simultaneously.

nibble Four bits, or half a byte.

operating system A comprehensive software package that acts as an intermediary between users and applications on the one hand, and the machine with its disk drives and other hardware devices on the other. *See also* **DOS**.

overlay files Files containing additional command and control information for sophisticated and complex programs. Large and seldom-used parts of programs can be placed in overlay files and loaded only as needed. This technique can reduce the overall memory requirements of an application program.

overwriting Typing new data over what is already there.

parameter An extra item of information, specified with a command, that determines how the command executes. With most DOS commands, the parameters are the names of files upon which the command is to operate. *See also* **literal, variable parameter**.

partition The section of a hard disk that contains an operating system. One hard disk can have up to four partitions.

password A sequence of characters that allows entry into a restricted system or program.

path The list of disks and directories that DOS will search to find a command file with a .COM, .BAT, or .EXE extension.

peripheral device Any physical device connected to the computer.

piping Redirecting the standard output of one program or command to the standard input of another program or command.

platter A rigid disk used in a hard-disk drive.

primary DOS partition Up to the first 32Mb of a hard disk. Contains the boot record and other DOS information files. *Compare with* **extended DOS partition**.

pull-down menus Menus that can be chosen from a bar along the top of the screen. Selection of an item typically displays a secondary menu.

RAM (random-access memory) The part of the computer's memory to which you have access; it stores programs and data while the computer is on. *See also* **memory, expanded memory, extended memory**.

RAM disk An area of RAM that you can use as if it were a disk drive. All data in this area of memory is lost when the computer is turned off or warm booted. Also known as a virtual disk. RAM disks are often created in extended memory. *See also* **extended memory**.

RAM-resident program *See* **TSR program**.

range A continuous series of values (minimum to maximum, first to last, and so on).

read-after-write verification An extra level of validity checking, invoked with the VERIFY command or the /V switch. In this method, DOS rereads data after writing it to a disk, comparing the written data to the original information.

read-only status Indicates that a file cannot be updated but can only be read.

read/write bit The bit in a file specification that indicates whether a file can accept changes or deletions or can only be accessed for reading.

read/write head A disk-drive mechanism that reads data from and writes data to a disk.

redirection Causing a program to receive input from a file or device other than the keyboard, or to send its output to a file or device other than the screen. *See also* **piping**.

resident command *See* **internal command**.

reverse video Black letters on an illuminated background.

root directory The first directory on any disk.

scrolling The up or down panning of your screen's display into a file (vertical scrolling). Also, the right or left panning of your screen's display (horizontal scrolling). Also, the action of a DOS screen when all twenty-five lines roll up one by one when a screen is full and a new line is displayed or entered.

sector A division of a disk track; usually, 512 bytes.

serial number A unique alphanumeric sequence assigned to each disk formatted by DOS 4. The code is physically stored in the boot sector of the disk and is used for identification and disk differentiation purposes by DOS 4.

Shift-PrtSc The DOS key combination that transfers an image of what is on the screen to the printer.

software The programs and instruction sets that operate the computer. *Compare with* **hardware**.

source The location containing the original data, files, or other information to be used in a DOS command. *Compare with* **destination**.

spindle The mechanism in a disk drive that holds and rotates the diskette or hard disk platters.

spooler The device or program that keeps track of files to be output.

spooling *S*imultaneous *p*eripheral *o*perations *o*n-*l*ine; the technique of using a high-speed disk to store input to or output from low-speed peripheral devices while the CPU performs other tasks.

streamer tape Thin, high-density tape used for backing up hard disks. Each streamer tape typically can hold 20 to 40 megabytes.

string A series of characters.

subdirectory A directory contained in another directory or subdirectory. Technically, all directories other than the root directory are subdirectories. *See also* **directory tree**.

switch A parameter included in a DOS command, usually a single letter preceded by the slash (/) symbol, whose predefined meaning modifies or further specifies the action of the command.

syntax The form and sequence in which you enter a command; includes spelling, parameter locations, and so on.

system disk A disk formatted to contain the DOS system files necessary to boot the system.

toggle A hardware switch or software command that changes a setting from one of its two possible states to the other.

track A circular section of a disk holding data. Similar to a track on a record, except that tracks on computer disks are not spiral.

transient command A command whose procedures are read from the disk into memory, executed from memory, and then erased from memory when finished. Also called external command.

TSR (terminate-and-stay-resident) A program that, when executed, carves out a piece of memory for itself and stays there. When you are done with the TSR program, it allows you to continue what you were previously doing. Also called a RAM-resident program.

utility program A supplemental routine or program designed to perform a specific operation, usually to modify the system environment or perform housekeeping tasks.

variable parameter A named element, following a command, that acts as a placeholder; when you issue the command, you replace the variable parameter with the actual value you want to use. *Compare with* **literal**.

VDISK.SYS Device driver used to create a RAM disk.

verbose listing A listing of all files and subdirectories contained on the disk and path specified in the command. Activated by the CHKDSK command with the /V switch.

virtual disk *See* **RAM disk**.

volume label A name, consisting of up to 11 characters, that can be assigned to any disk during a DOS FORMAT operation or after formatting with the LABEL command.

warm booting Resetting the computer using the Ctrl-Alt-Del key combination. *See also* **bootstrapping, cold booting**.

wide directory listing An alternate output format that lists file names in five columns.

wildcards Characters used to represent other characters. In DOS, * and ? are the only wildcard symbols. The question mark represents a single character, and the asterisk represents any number of characters.

word A unit of computer storage, typically two bytes in PC usage.

word processor An application program that allows the creation, correction and reformatting of documents before they are printed. Most of the common word processing programs work with DOS. Occasionally, a computer system is designed to be used exclusively for word processing. Such systems do not use DOS.

write-protection Technique that gives a disk read-only status by covering the write-protect notch. Also, a feature of the ATTRIB command that, when set, allows files to be read from, but not written to.

APPENDIX B

Hard Disk Error and Information Messages

This appendix lists all DOS hard-disk related messages in alphabetical order, showing the cause of the error or information message and solutions or actions to take to rectify the error or satisfy the message, if any exist.

Access denied

Cause: You tried to access a file incorrectly (for example, you tried to write to a read-only file).

Response: Use another file or change the attributes of the file you tried to access; then try the operation again.

Add *d:\ path\ filename?*

Cause: When you executed REPLACE, you asked to be prompted. This message asks whether you want the file added to the target disk.

Response: Reply Y or N, and then press ↵.

Adding *d:\ path\ filename*

Cause: REPLACE is adding the specified file to the target.

Response: No response required.

All available space in the Extended DOS Partition is assigned to logical drives.

Cause: Your extended partition is used up, and has no more remaining space.

Response: Reduce the size of one or more existing logical drives. Then rerun FDISK to create the desired new logical drive.

All files in directory will be deleted!
Are you sure (Y/N)?

Cause: You tried to erase all files in a directory, usually with a wildcard specification.

Response: Enter a Y to complete the deletion; enter an N to withdraw the request.

All logical drives deleted in the Extended DOS partition

Cause: You deleted all of the defined drives in the extended DOS partition on your hard disk.

Response: No response required. You can now delete the extended DOS partition, if you wish.

All specified file(s) are contiguous

Cause: None of the files on the specified disk are fragmented.

Response: No response required.

Allocation error, size adjusted

Cause: An incorrect cluster number appears in the file-allocation table.

Response: If you entered CHKDSK, type CHKDSK/F to correct the file size.

x allocation units available on disk
x bytes in each allocation unit

Cause: The FORMAT command indicates how many clusters are available on the disk, and how many bytes are consumed by each cluster (allocation unit).

Response: No response necessary.

APPEND already installed

Cause: You tried to execute APPEND from a disk when it was already loaded into memory.

Response: Execute APPEND from memory by not preceding it with a drive or path specification.

APPEND / ASSIGN conflict

Cause: You tried to load APPEND after ASSIGN had been executed.

Response: Load APPEND first and then ASSIGN.

APPEND / TopView conflict

Cause: You tried executing APPEND after entering TopView.

Response: Exit TopView, execute APPEND, and then return to TopView.

Attempt to remove current directory

Cause: You tried to remove the current directory.

Response: Change to another directory (using CD), make sure the target directory is empty of files, and then try again to remove it.

Attempting to recover allocation unit *x*

Cause: Bad clusters are encountered during the FORMAT process.

Response: No response necessary.

Attempted write-protect violation

Cause: You are trying to format a write-protected diskette.

Response: Insert a new diskette or remove the write-protect label on the current diskette.

*** Backing up files to drive *x* *** Diskette Number: *n*

Cause: BACKUP is displaying the names of the files it is currently processing.

Response: No response required.

Backup file sequence error

Cause: You inserted a diskette out of sequence for a file that is backed up on several diskettes.

Response: Restart RESTORE and use the correct diskette order.

Bad command or file name

Cause: You entered an invalid command or misspelled a file name.

Response: Check your spelling. If you are trying to execute a batch file, check the path and your current directory.

Bad Partition Table

Cause: The fixed disk does not have a DOS partition or the partition is invalid.

Response: Use FDISK to create a new DOS partition and reenter FORMAT.

Batch file missing

Cause: DOS cannot find the batch file it was executing because the PATH was changed; the file was moved, renamed, or deleted; or the current drive was changed. This error is fatal and terminates batch processing.

Response: Include drive letters in your path or correct any commands that in any way alter the characteristics of the batch file in which they exist.

Buffer size adjusted

Cause: VDISK changed the size of the buffer in the line DEVICE=VDISK.SYS in CONFIG.SYS.

Response: No response required.

Buffer size:
Sector size:
Directory entries:
Transfer size:

Cause: When VDISK is invoked, this message appears to show how the virtual disk was set up.

Response: No response required.

Cannot CHDIR to root

Cause: While trying to change to the root directory, CHKDSK detected damage to the disk and was unable to perform its operation.

Response: Back up whatever you can from the disk; use RECOVER or the Norton Utilities to restore whatever you can and then back up those files; reformat the disk and then recreate your file directory structure.

Cannot CHKDSK a network drive

Cause: CHKDSK does not work on network or shared drives.

Response: Pause the server, execute a CHKDSK command, and then continue server operation.

Cannot CHKDSK a SUBSTed or ASSIGNed drive

Cause: CHKDSK cannot find information it needs when SUBST is in effect.

Response: Deactivate SUBST.

Cannot create Extended DOS Partition without primary DOS partition on disk 1

Cause: You must have a primary DOS partition on the first fixed disk drive.

Response: Create a primary DOS partition on the disk using FDISK and then create an extended partition.

Cannot create a zero size partition

Cause: You tried to create a partition with no size (0 cylinders).

Response: When you create a partition, specify a size of at least 1 cylinder.

Cannot create logical DOS drive without an extended DOS partition on the current drive

Cause: You tried to create a new logical drive on a physical drive that has not been partitioned properly.

Response: Using FDISK, create an extended DOS partition on the target drive. Then try again to create a new logical drive.

Cannot delete extended DOS partition while logical drives exist

Cause: You tried to remove an extended DOS partition that still had logical drives defined for it.

Response: Using FDISK, remove all of the logical drives from the extended partition; then delete the extended partition.

Cannot delete primary DOS partition on drive 1 when an extended DOS partition exists

Cause: You tried to remove a primary DOS partition while an extended partition still remains.

Response: Using FDISK, delete the extended partition first.

Cannot execute FORMAT

Cause: You tried to make a backup copy on an unformatted floppy disk. BACKUP therefore needs to format the disk, but it cannot find FORMAT in the current directory or along the path.

Response: Replace the unformatted diskette with a formatted diskette and press a key, or restart BACKUP making sure the FORMAT command is available. DOS 3.X users should remember to use the /F switch when invoking the FORMAT command.

Cannot FDISK with network loaded

Cause: You tried to use FDISK on a networked hard disk.

Response: Restart the system and execute FDISK before loading the network software.

Cannot find FORMAT.COM

Cause: You used an unformatted diskette during the BACKUP process, and the FORMAT.COM file was not accessible in the current directory or on the PATH.

Response: In order to continue the BACKUP process, insert a formatted diskette. Or, abort the current backup procedure, make sure that FORMAT-.COM is accessible, and then restart BACKUP. DOS 3.X users should remember to use the /F switch when invoking the FORMAT command.

Cannot find System Files

Cause: FORMAT could not find the hidden system files.

Response: Change to a drive with the system files on it.

Cannot FORMAT a Network drive

Cause: You cannot use FORMAT with a network or shared drive.

Response: In sharing situations, pause the server, execute FORMAT, and then continue server operation.

Cannot format an ASSIGNed or SUBSTed drive

Cause: You tried to format a disk with an ASSIGN or SUBST command in effect.

Response: Type ASSIGN to remove the assignments and then format the disk.

Cannot FORMAT nonremovable drive *x*

Cause: When you executed BACKUP, you used the /F option. You can use this option only on diskettes and nonnetwork drives.

Response: Terminate the BACKUP operation and prepare the hard disk with FORMAT; then reexecute the BACKUP command.

Cannot JOIN a network drive

Cause: You tried to use JOIN with a network drive.

Response: No response required.

Cannot LABEL a network drive

Cause: You tried to change the volume label on a block device that has been redirected.

Response: No response required.

Cannot LABEL a SUBSTed or ASSIGNed drive

Cause: You tried to write a label onto a disk that has previously run an ASSIGN or SUBST command.

Response: No response required.

Cannot make directory entry

Cause: DOS attempted on your behalf to make a new file entry in a disk directory, but the disk is full, or the directory table is full.

Response: Delete one or more files from the desired directory or run CHKDSK to analyze the disk.

Cannot perform a cyclic copy

Cause: You incorrectly specified the /S parameter in a copy operation so that the destination was a file or directory already included as part of the source.

Response: Change source and target directories as needed, and reissue the XCOPY command.

Cannot recover entry, processing continued

Cause: A serious FAT chaining error has occurred: The FAT chain of clusters is corrupted.

Response: Use a data recovery program like the Norton Utilities to attempt to recover as much as possible of the file. Otherwise, delete the file name and restore an earlier backup version.

Cannot read file allocation table

Cause: RECOVER cannot successfully read the disk's FAT.

Response: FORMAT the disk again.

Cannot recover .. entry

Cause: The /F parameter was specified, but the current (.) and parent (..) directories cannot be fixed.

Response: No response necessary.

Cannot recover .. entry, processing continued

Cause: The /F parameter was specified, but the current (.) and parent (..) directories cannot be fixed.

Response: No response necessary.

Cannot RECOVER a network drive

Cause: RECOVER cannot be used on a shared network drive.

Response: In a sharing situation, pause the server, execute RECOVER, then continue server operation.

Cannot RECOVER an ASSIGNed or SUBSTed drive

Cause: RECOVER cannot be used on drives that have been ASSIGNed, SUBSTed, or JOINed.

Response: Remove the ASSIGNment, SUBSTitution, or JOIN. Then run RECOVER again.

Cannot use FASTOPEN for drive *x*

Cause: You attempted to use FASTOPEN on a joined, assigned, substituted, or floppy drive.

Response: Undo any drive or directory reassignments.

Cannot SUBST a network drive

Cause: You tried to use SUBST with a network drive or path.

Response: Use PAUSE if you must establish the substitution.

Cannot XCOPY from a reserved device

Cause: You tried to execute XCOPY from a character device (a printer or communication port).

Response: Copy the data you need into a file and then use that file as the source for your XCOPY command.

Cannot XCOPY to a reserved device

Cause: You tried to execute XCOPY to a character device (printer, communication port, or NULL). As a reserved device name in DOS, NULL is equivalent to a waste basket; DOS discards any information sent to that device.

Response: Specify a block or file device instead of a character device and reexecute XCOPY.

CHKDSK..failed, trying alternate method

Cause: CHKDSK encountered an unrecoverable error during a subdirectory data read or write.

Response: Reboot and execute CHKDSK again.

Color file missing or unreadable

Cause: The SHELL.CLR file is inaccessible.

Response: Place a copy of SHELL.CLR in the directory containing the DOS shell program, then run DOSSHELL again.

Compare error at OFFSET *x*

Cause: This message displays in hexadecimal notation the offset location where the two files to be compared differ.

Response: No response required.

Compare more files (Y/N)?

Cause: This message asks whether you want to compare more diskettes after one COMP operation is complete.

Response: Enter Y to compare more files or N to exit COMP.

Configuration too large for memory

Cause: This message appears when the FILES and BUFFERS commands in the CONFIG.SYS file, or the resetting of the environment space, do not leave enough memory for COMMAND-.COM to be reloaded.

Response: Reboot with a different disk and then change the values to leave enough memory for COMMAND.COM.

Contains *x* non-contiguous blocks

Cause: This message indicates the number of pieces into which a file is fragmented.

Response: No response required. However, the existence of many fragmented files slows down disk operations. Copying files to another disk will combine the fragments and speed up future file access operations.

Contents of destination lost before copy

Cause: The target file has the same name as one of the input filenames specified.

Response: No response necessary. The one source file of the same name is skipped during the multiple file merging process.

Convert directory to file (Y/N)?

Cause: The displayed directory has much bad information and cannot effectively be used as a directory.

Response: Type Y to convert the directory to a file so that you can check it; type N if you do not want to convert the directory to a file.

x lost clusters found in *y* chains. Convert lost chains to files (Y/N)?

Cause: While another program was accessing the disk, the system was turned off or Ctrl-Break was pressed, scrambling the file being accessed. CHKDSK asks you if you wish it to clean up this scrambling.

Response: As long as the /F switch is in effect, type Y to clean up the disk and allow the scrambled blocks to be used by other files. If /F was not invoked, CHKDSK will display information messages only, doing nothing to the disk. In that case you can answer N and then reissue the CHKDSK /F command.

Current drive is no longer valid

Cause: You deleted the network drive, and the prompt setting needs to determine what drive you are using.

Response: Move to a valid drive.

Data error

Cause: A disk has gone bad in part or completely. Sectors are either unreadable or unwritable.

Response: FORMAT the disk again, saving any critical information already on the disk before doing so.

d: drive deleted

Cause: This message appears during deletion of a logical drive in an extended DOS partition.

Response: No response required.

Delete (Y/N)?

Cause: You used the /P switch when you specified filenames to erase.

Response: Enter Y to delete the displayed file, or N not to delete it.

Delete current volume label (Y/N)?

Cause: You attempted to enter a new volume label when one already exists.

Response: Enter Y to delete the current volume label or N not to delete it.

Dir path listing for volume *x*

Cause: This message displays the volume label of the disk.

Response: No response required.

Directory already exists

Cause: Attempting to create a directory of the same name as an existing directory.

Response: Try again, using a different directory name.

Directory entries adjusted

Cause: VDISK changed the number of directory entries in the DEVICE=VDISK.SYS statement in the CONFIG.SYS file.

Response: No response required.

Directory is joined,
tree past this point not processed

Cause: CHKDSK did not check a directory that is actually a joined drive.

Response: In order to use CHKDSK further, you must disjoin (/D) the drive from the directory tree, then use CHKDSK explicitly on that physically separate drive.

Directory is totally empty, no . or ..,
tree past this point not processed

Cause: DOS found a directory that does not contain the . and .. files. These files may have been left out (by DOS) during an updating operation that was interrupted.

Response: Use RECOVER to try to restore the damaged files.

Directory not empty

Cause: Attempting to join a directory that is not empty.

Response: Respecify an empty directory.

Disk error reading FAT *n*

Cause: Your file-allocation table is invalid (perhaps because of a power failure during a file access).

Response: If both FAT 1 and FAT 2 generate this message, reformat the disk. If the formatting fails, the disk is bad and you must use a new disk.

Disk error writing FAT *n*

Cause: Your file-allocation table is invalid and cannot write data.

Response: If both FAT 1 and FAT 2 generate this message, reformat the disk. If the formatting fails, the disk is bad and you must use a new disk.

Disk full error writing to BACKUP Log File

Cause: Target disk for the log information during the BACKUP process has become full.

Response: Press a key to continue the BACKUP processing, or press Ctrl-Break to restart.

Disk not compatible

Cause: You are trying to format a disk under DOS in a drive not supported by DOS.

Response: Use a DOS-supported drive.

Disk unsuitable for system disk

Cause: A bad track was found at the location to which DOS files needed to be copied.

Response: The current disk cannot contain DOS, but can hold data. Use another disk for DOS.

Do you wish to use the maximum size for a DOS partition and make the DOS partition active (Y/N).....[ ]

Cause: This request appears when you select suboption 1 of the Create Primary DOS Partition option.

Response: Answer Y to have the primary DOS partition occupy the largest possible amount of space on the disk to 32 megabytes and to mark that partition as active. Answer N to select another partition size.

Does not exist

Cause: Invalid directory, or invalid sector data.

Response: Use the /F switch, and rerun CHKDSK to correct the possible problem.

Does *pathname* specify a file name or directory name on the target (F = file, D = directory)?

Cause: When using XCOPY, you did not specify an existing directory for your specified destination

Response: Answer D to create the specified directory; answer F if you are copying only one file and do not wish to create a directory.

DOS partition already exists

Cause: A partition for DOS already exists.

Response: Choose a different FDISK option from the options screen.

Drive *d*: already deleted

Cause: The logical drive you are trying to delete has already been deleted.

Response: No response required.

Drive letter must be specified

Cause: You did not specify a drive to be formatted.

Response: Reenter the command specifying the drive to be formatted.

Drive letters have been changed or deleted

Cause: Some logical drives in the extended partition have been deleted, possibly causing the remaining logical drives to be renumbered.

Response: Note the new drive numbers for future reference.

Duplicate file name or file not found

Cause: The file to be renamed could not be found, the file name you specified for renaming already exists as another file, or you are renaming a file with the same name.

Response: Check your spelling and verify the names you are using; then retry the command.

Enter current Volume Label for Drive *d*:

Cause: You have tried to FORMAT your hard disk, which would mean losing any information—data and programs—stored on it. To prevent you from doing this accidentally, FORMAT requires you to enter the hard disk's volume label.

Response: Enter the hard disk's volume label if you wish to format the hard disk.

Enter partition size...........: [*d*]

Cause: You need to specify the size of the partition you wish to create.

Response: Press Enter to make the number shown in brackets the partition size. To specify a different size, enter a new number.

Enter primary file name

Cause: You need to enter a primary file name.

Response: Specify the filespec of one of the two files to be compared.

Enter 2nd file name or drive id

Cause: You need to specify the second of the two files to be compared.

Response: Specify the filespec of the second file to be compared.

Enter the number of the partition you want to make active.........: [ ]

Cause: You are using the "Change Active Partition" option and need to specify the partition to be activated.

Response: Enter the number of the partition to be activated.

Entry has a bad attribute (or size or link)

Cause: A directory entry contains an error. If the message is preceded by a period, the current directory contains the error. If the message is preceded by two periods, the parent directory contains the error.

Response: Run CHKDSK using the /F parameter to change the damaged directory.

Eof mark not found

Cause: While comparing nontext files, COMP could not find the end-of-file marker in a file.

Response: No response required.

Error executing FORMAT

Cause: BACKUP is unable to execute the FORMAT command to prepare an unformatted disk. Your system probably does not have enough memory.

Response: Change the BUFFERS value in your CONFIG.SYS file. Then restart DOS and try BACKUP again.

Error found, F parameter not specified Corrections will not be written to disk

Cause: An error was detected somewhere on the disk. Since you did not specify the /F parameter when you invoked CHKDSK, CHKDSK will perform the error analysis and simulate a solution, but will not change anything on the disk.

Response: To correct the problem, reexecute the command using the /F parameter.

Error loading operating system

Cause: An error appeared when you attempted to load the operating system from your hard disk.

Response: Reboot. If the error still occurs, recopy the system to your hard disk and reexecute processing.

Error opening log file

Cause: An error occurred during the requested opening or creation of a backup log file. The error may result from an invalid drive or path specification, a file-sharing conflict, or a lack of appropriate directory entries in the root directory.

Response: Check your log-file specification. Be sure that you are not attempting to create the log file on the destination disk.

Error reading directory

Cause: Bad sectors in the specified directory or in the disk's file allocation table.

Response: Try reformatting your disk after copying any important files from that disk to another.

Error reading fixed disk

Cause: After trying five times, FDISK still could not read the startup record of the hard disk.

Response: Retry FDISK several times. If the error recurs every time, consult you computer's user's manual or contact your local dealer for assistance.

Error reading partition table

Cause: An error occurred during a partition table read operation.

Response: Rerun FDISK.

Error writing directory

Cause: Bad sectors in the specified directory or in the disk's file allocation table.

Response: Try reformatting your disk after copying any important files from that disk to another.

Error writing FAT

Cause: Disk error occurred during FORMAT's update of the file allocation table.

Response: Try reformatting your disk after copying any important files from that disk to another.

Error writing fixed disk

Cause: After trying five times, FDISK still could not write the startup record of the hard disk.

Cause: Retry FDISK several times. If the error is regenerated every time, consult your computer's user manual or contact your dealer.

Error writing partition table

Cause: An error occurred during a partition table write operation.

Response: Rerun FDISK.

Errors found, F parameter not specified Corrections will not be written to disk

Cause: Structural errors were discovered on the disk, but they will not be corrected because the /F fixup parameter was not specified.

Response: Rerun the CHKDSK command with the /F parameter.

EXEC failure

Cause: An error occurred when DOS tried to read a command from the disk because the FILES= statement in the CONFIG.SYS file was not set to a sufficiently large value.

Response: Change the FILES= value and reboot. If the problem persists, the disk itself may contain a hardware error.

Extended DOS partition already exists

Cause: There can only be one extended DOS partition per hard disk.

Response: No response required. Use the Display Partition Information option on the FDISK main menu to see what partitions have been set up.

Extended DOS partition deleted

Cause: This message confirms the deletion of the extended DOS partition and everything in it.

Response: No response required.

Extender card switches do not match the system memory size

Cause: The settings on your memory extended card do not match the total system memory value. VDISK does not use memory that is in an expansion unit.

Response: Verify your extended card switch settings.

FASTOPEN already installed

Cause: You tried to load FASTOPEN again.

Response: To reload FASTOPEN, you must reboot.

FASTOPEN EMS entry count exceeded. Use fewer entries

Cause: You tried to load FASTOPEN in extended memory, but insufficient space exists for your specified parameter values.

Response: Rerun FASTOPEN with smaller setup values.

FASTOPEN installed

Cause: FASTOPEN was successfully loaded and executed.

Response: No response required.

FCB unavailable

Cause: The FCBS command, while file sharing was loaded, did not specify enough FCBs to be open.

Response: Redefine the FCBS command in the CONFIG.SYS file and reboot.

File allocation table bad, drive *x*

Cause: You are attempting to read absolute sectors on a network drive.

Response: Use the Loader Write *filespec* option of the DEBUG command.

File *x* canceled by operator

Cause: This message is output to the printer when you cancel printing to remind whoever reads the printout that the output was interrupted and that the printout may be incomplete.

Response: No response required.

File cannot be copied onto itself

Cause: You attempted to copy a file onto itself.

Response: Modify the destination *filespec* so that it contains a different directory and name.

File creation error

Cause: A file could not be created or renamed.

Response: Check the attributes of the file to make sure you are not renaming or changing a read-only file. Use CHKDSK to determine whether the directory is full or whether something else is wrong.

File not found

Cause: DOS or a particular command could not find a specified file.

Response: Check the spelling of your specification. Make sure the indicated file is where it is supposed to be. If it is not, move it.

File not in PRINT queue

Cause: You tried to cancel a file in the print queue that is not actually in the print queue.

Response: Check the spelling of your specification and reexecute processing.

File sharing conflict

Cause: You tried to compare two files while one of the

files was being used (and hence locked) by another process.

Response: Reissue COMP later, when the file is available.

Files compare OK

Cause: This message appears after a successful comparison of two files.

Response: No response required.

*** Files were backed up *xx/xx/xxxx* ***

Cause: This message displays the date the files on the backup diskettes were backed up.

Response: No response required.

First cluster number is invalid, entry is truncated

Cause: Invalid pointer exists for this file. If you ran CHKDSK with /F before seeing this message, the file has been truncated to length 0.

Response: No response necessary.

Fixed backup device *d:* is full

Cause: The hard disk you are attempting to back up files onto is full.

Response: Make space on the hard disk or back up onto another disk.

Format failure

Cause: The disk to be formatted is unusable.

Response: Use or buy another disk.

FORMAT not supported on drive *d*

Cause: The disk device driver (probably a RAM disk) does not support or require formatting.

Response: Resubmit the FORMAT command for a different disk drive identifier.

Has invalid cluster, file truncated

Cause: The specified file contains an invalid data-area pointer.

Response: Use the /F parameter to truncate the file at the last valid data block.

Help file missing or unreadable

Cause: The SHELL.HLP file is inaccessible.

Response: Place a copy of SHELL.HLP in the directory containing the DOS shell program.

Incorrect APPEND version

Cause: You initially loaded a version of APPEND that is different than the one you are trying to use now.

Response: Verify your path setting or determine why you are calling a different APPEND version and rectify the problem. You may have started with the network APPEND command and are now using a local version.

Incorrect DOS version

Cause: You are currently running a version of DOS that does not support the command (or the version of the command) you want to use.

Response: Make sure you are using commands for the specific version of DOS that you are using. If you are on a network, reset the path to access a local version of DOS that has the correct version for the command you want to use.

Incorrect startup option

Cause: One of the many switch options on the DOSSHELL command is specified or spelled incorrectly.

Response: Check all specified switches for spelling and for correctness on your system's version of DOS 4.

Insert backup diskette *x* in drive *x*: Press any key when ready

Cause: You need to insert the specified diskette to continue restoring your data.

Response: Insert the specified diskette and press a key to continue.

Insert backup source diskette in drive *x* Strike any key when ready

Cause: You need to insert the specified diskette to continue backing up your files.

Response: Insert the specified diskette and press a key to continue.

Insert backup target diskette *y* in drive *x* Strike any key when ready

Cause: You need to insert the next diskette, so that the backup operation can continue.

Response: Insert the specified diskette and press a key to continue.

Insert DOS diskette in drive A:
Press any key when ready...

Cause: A DOS partition was successfully created on the current hard disk.

Response: Insert the requested disk and press a key to reboot the system. You can now format the partition.

Insert last backup diskette in drive *x*

Cause: You specified the /A parameter.

Response: Insert the last backup target diskette used in the last backup operation and press a key to continue.

Insert new diskette for drive *x*
and press ENTER when ready

Cause: You need to insert the disk you wish to have formatted in the specified drive.

Response: Insert the specified diskette in drive *x* and press a key to continue formatting.

Insert restore target *x* in drive *y*
Strike any key when ready

Cause: This prompt asks you to insert the diskette to be restored in a drive.

Response: Insert the specified disk in the specified drive and press a key to continue.

Insufficient disk space

Cause: The disk does not have enough free space to store your file.

Response: Run CHKDSK to make sure this message is valid. If it is, use another diskette, or delete files on the current diskette to make more room.

Insufficient memory for system transfer

Cause: Not enough memory is available to allow the transfer of the system files.

Response: Change the BUFFERS = command in the CONFIG.SYS file to a lower value. If the message reappears, you need to obtain more memory. Be aware that TSR programs consume memory; removing one or more of these programs from memory may solve the problem.

Insufficient room in root directory
Erase files from root directory and repeat CHKDSK

Cause: CHKDSK could not recover all of the lost chains into files because not enough space was available in the root directory.

Response: Review the recovered files, deleting or relocating the ones you can, and rerun CHKDSK to recover the remaining chains.

Intermediate file error during pipe

Cause: Either one or both of the intermediate pipe files could not be created due to a full root directory, the inability of DOS to find the piping files, or the lack of enough disk space to hold the piped data.

Response: Make room in the default drive root directory by erasing some files; then reissue the command.

Invalid characters in volume label

Cause: You entered characters for the volume label that are not valid label characters. The characters * / \ | . , ; : + = < > [ ] ( ) @ ^ cannot be used in a volume label. The length of the name must be between 1 and 11 characters.

Response: Reissue the command using valid characters and a name of the right length.

Invalid current directory

Cause: An unrecoverable disk error occurred during a read operation for the current directory.

Response: Use a disk utilities package to ascertain the exact nature of the problem and a possible remedy for it.

Invalid device parameters from device driver

Cause: The number of hidden sectors is not an exact multiple of the number of sectors per track, or the DOS partition appears not to start on a track boundary.

Response: Use FDISK to create a new partition and then reexecute FORMAT.

Invalid directory

Cause: You named a nonexistent directory in the path specification, possibly by a simple misspelling.

Response: Respecify the path.

Invalid drive in search path

Cause: You named an invalid drive identifier in the path specification, possibly by a simple misspelling.

Response: Respecify the path using a valid drive identifier.

Invalid drive or file name

Cause: You specified an invalid drive or file name.

Response: Reissue the command with valid specifications.

Invalid drive specification

Cause: You entered an invalid drive identifier, or the source and target drive specifications in a command are the same.

Response: Enter the correct identifiers.

Invalid file name or file not found

Cause: You used an invalid or nonexistent file name, possibly by a simple misspelling, or you used global characters in a TYPE command.

Response: Reissue the command correctly, adding paths if necessary.

Invalid extent entry

Cause: You used an invalid cache value (second parameter), less than 0 or greater than 999.

Response: Reissue the command with parameter values in the range 1 to 999.

Invalid file/directory entry

Cause: You used an invalid file/directory entry value (first parameter), less than 10 or greater than 999.

Response: Reissue the command with a parameter value in the range 10 to 999.

Invalid media or Track 0 bad—disk unusable

Cause: Track 0 could not be formatted, indicating a bad disk, or the disk and drive types are mismatched.

Response: If track 0 is the problem, use or buy another disk. Otherwise, place a correct disk in the drive.

Invalid partition table

Cause: During startup, DOS found invalid information in the partition information area.

Response: Reboot DOS from diskette and use FDISK to fix any errors in the partition definitions.

Invalid path

Cause: You entered a path with invalid characters, an invalid file name, or more than 63 characters.

Response: Check your spelling and reissue the command in the correct format with the correct information.

Invalid path, not directory or directory not empty

Cause: You did not specify a valid directory name in the path; the directory to be removed still contains entries for other files and subdirectories, or you are trying to remove the current directory.

Response: Check your spelling and enter a valid directory name, empty the directory you wish removed, or change to a different directory and reexecute processing.

Invalid path or file not found

Cause: You specified a nonexistent file or directory, possibly by a simple misspelling.

Response: Check your spelling, the file name, and the availability of files before reissuing the command.

Invalid path or file name

Cause: You specified a non-existent directory or filename.

Response: Correct the spelling, or specify a different name in the command string.

Invalid subdirectory entry

Cause: CHKDSK found invalid data in the specified subdirectory.

Response: Use the /F or /V parameters when invoking CHKDSK.

Invalid Volume ID

Cause: You entered a volume label different from that of the disk.

Response: Enter the VOL command to determine the current volume label.

x is cross linked on cluster *n*

Cause: The same disk cluster is allocated to two different files.

Response: Copy both files to other locations, erase the filenames, then see which one (if either) is retrievable, in part or completely.

Last backup diskette not inserted

Cause: You specified the /A parameter on the command line, but the target disk was not the last disk of the backup set.

Response: No response required.

*** Last file not backed up ***

Cause: While you were backing up to a hard disk, the hard disk became full, and the most recently backed-up file was not saved on the hard disk. This message also indicates a possible file-sharing error.

Response: Delete files on the target disk and rerun the BACKUP command.

Lock Violation

Cause: While trying to read files on a network, XCOPY encountered one or more files that were locked against reading.

Response: Wait a few moments and reexecute the command. Continue this procedure until you gain access to the file or decide to do without the locked file.

Logging to file *x*

Cause: This message occurs when you specify the /L parameter. File *x* is the log file to which information about the backup is being written.

Response: No response required.

Logical DOS drive created, drive letters changed or added

Cause: You created a logical DOS drive, and it was assigned a drive identifier.

Response: No response required. Before you use the drive, however, you must format it.

Maximum available space for partition is *x* cylinders

Cause: This message tells you how much space is available for a partition when you choose the Create DOS Partition option.

Response: No response required.

Maximum number of logical DOS drives installed

Cause: All available drive letters have been assigned.

Response: To create a new drive, delete a current drive to free a letter.

Menu file missing or unreadable

Cause: The SHELL.MEU file is inaccessible.

Response: Copy the SHELL.MEU file to the directory containing the DOSSHELL program. Then restart DOSSHELL.

Missing operating system

Cause: The boot area of your fixed disk, when started, does not contain a valid DOS boot record.

Response: Reboot using a diskette. Use FORMAT/S to install DOS on the hard disk or use SYS. If you use FORMAT, back up your files first, as they will be erased.

Mouse file missing or unreadable

Cause: The mouse driver file is inaccessible, although the DOS shell was brought up with the /MOS switch.

Response: Copy the appropriate mouse driver file to the directory containing the DOSSHELL program. Then restart DOSSHELL.

No Append

Cause: APPEND has no directories specified.

Response: No response required.

No Extended DOS partition to delete

Cause: FDISK cannot delete the extended DOS partition because it does not exist.

Response: No response required.

No files added

Cause: You invoked REPLACE with the /A parameter, but all of the source files already exist in the target directory.

Response: No response required.

No files found

Cause: REPLACE could find no source files in the specified directory or along the specified path.

Response: No response required.

No fixed disks present

Cause: FDISK could find no hard-disk drive attached to the computer. This could be because of improper installation or because you did not turn on your expansion unit.

Response: Make sure the expansion unit is turned on; then determine the cause of the problem and correct it.

No free file handles
Cannot start COMMAND, exiting

Cause: Too many files are currently open to allow the loading of a secondary command processor.

Response: Close some files in one of your running application programs or increase the value of the FILES= command in the CONFIG.SYS file and reboot.

No logical drives defined

Cause: You have not defined any logical drives in the extended partition.

Response: Use FDISK to create the logical drives and then use FORMAT to format them.

No partitions defined

Cause: You have not defined any partitions on the hard disk.

Response: Use FDISK to set up some partitions and divide them into logical drives; then use FORMAT to format them.

No partitions to delete

Cause: You tried to delete partitions, but none have been defined.

Response: No response required.

No partitions to make active

Cause: You cannot change the active partition because no partitions have been defined.

Response: Define one or more partitions and make one active.

No Path

Cause: You have not specified a path to search.

Response: Use the PATH command to define a path.

No Primary DOS partition to delete

Cause: You tried to delete a nonexistent partition.

Response: Reenter the deletion request, specifying a valid partition.

No source drive specified

Cause: You did not specify a source-drive parameter.

Response: Specify both source and destination drives and reexecute processing.

No space to create a DOS partition

Cause: You tried to create a DOS partition, but there is no room left on the current disk to create another partition.

Response: Reduce the size of the existing partitions.

No subdirectories exist

Cause: The drive you wish to examine does not contain directories other than the root directory.

Response: No response required.

No system on default drive

Cause: The disk from which you are trying to copy the system does not contain the operating system files.

Response: Use a source disk that contains the system files.

No target drive specified

Cause: When invoking a command, you did not specify the target drive.

Response: Reissue the command with the correct parameters.

Non-System disk or disk error
Replace and strike any key when ready

Cause: The hidden files IBMBIO.COM and IBMDOS-.COM could not be located on the disk that you used to boot the system, or an error occurred while the system tried to read information from the disk during booting.

Response: Use a different DOS diskette for booting.

*** Not able to back up file ***

Cause: A file-sharing conflict occurred during backup processing.

Response: Reissue the command after a few moments, using the /M parameter.

**** Not able to restore file ***

Cause: A file-sharing conflict occurred during the restore process.

Response: Reissue the command after a few moments.

Only non-startable partitions exist

Cause: While defining partitions on your hard disk, you did not define an active partition containing the system files and boot information.

Response: Repartition the disk with a primary DOS partition.

Only partitions on Drive 1 can be made active

Cause: Since the system can be booted only from the first hard disk, you do not need to specify any active partitions on other drives.

Response: No response required.

Parameters not compatible

Cause: You tried to use format parameters that are invalid for the specified media or that are incompatible with each other.

Response: Check the parameter switches selected, and reissue the command correctly.

Partition selected (#) is not startable, active partition not changed

Cause: You attempted to activate a partition that cannot be booted.

Response: Reissue the command specifying a bootable partition.

Partition *x* made active

Cause: You have successfully made partition *x* the active partition.

Response: No response required.

Path not found

Cause: You specified an invalid path or directory on the command line.

Response: Use the correct information and reissue your command.

Path too long

Cause: You specified a path on the command line that exceeded the maximum length of 63 characters.

Response: Reissue the command with a path of the right length.

Please insert volume *x serial a-b*

Cause: A diskette was removed from a drive while files were still open.

Response: Put that diskette back into the drive.

Press any key to begin adding file(s)

Cause: REPLACE is giving you time to insert the correct disk or to change your mind and abort the process.

Response: Press a key when you are ready to continue.

Press any key to begin copying file(s)

Cause: XCOPY is giving you time to insert the correct disk or to decide to cancel the XCOPY request.

Response: Press a key to continue.

Press any key to begin recovery of the file(s) on drive *x*

Cause: RECOVER is giving you time to insert the correct disk or to decide to cancel the recovery request.

Response: Insert the specified disk and press a key to continue.

Press any key to begin replacing file(s)

Cause: REPLACE is giving you time to insert the correct disk or to decide to cancel the recovery request.

Response: Insert the correct diskettes, as needed, and then press any key to continue.

Primary DOS partition already exists

Cause: You have already defined a primary DOS partition on the current hard disk.

Response: No response required.

Primary DOS partition created

Cause: The primary DOS partition has been created and assigned a drive letter.

Response: You must now format the partition.

Primary DOS partition deleted

Cause: You have successfully deleted the primary DOS partition and its contents from the disk.

Response: No response required.

Print queue is empty

Cause: PRINT is not printing any files.

Response: No response required.

Print queue is full

Cause: You sent a file to the print queue, but exceeded the limit on the number of files that the queue can hold.

Response: Wait for one of the files in the queue to be printed; then retransmit your file.

Probable non-DOS disk
Continue (Y/N)?

Cause: The file-allocation table is bad, or the disk was not formatted.

Response: Use the /F parameter to correct the problem or reformat the disk.

Replace <*d:path\ filename*> (Y/N)?

Cause: You need to confirm a replacement.

Response: Enter Y to replace the file; enter N not to replace the file.

Replacing <*d:path\ filename*)

Cause: This message indicates which file is being replaced.

Response: No response required.

Requested logical drive size exceeds the maximum available space

Cause: You specified a drive size larger than the space left in the extended DOS partition.

Response: Specify a new, smaller drive size.

Requested partition size exceeds the maximum available space

Cause: You specified a partition size larger than the space left on the disk.

Response: Specify a new, smaller partition size.

Restore file sequence error

Cause: You did not insert the diskettes in the right order, so files were not restored.

Response: Reissue the RESTORE command, this time inserting the disks in the correct order.

***** Restoring files from drive *x* *****

Cause: This message lists the files that were restored.

Response: No response required.

***** Restoring files from drive *y* ***
Source *x***

Cause: Source files are being restored.

Response: No response required.

Same drive specified more than once

Cause: You specified the same drive identifier twice on the FASTOPEN command line.

Response: Reissue the FASTOPEN command using each drive identifier only once.

Sector not found

Cause: A data sector on the disk could not be found.

Response: Reenter the command. If the error recurs, abort the command and use a different diskette.

Sector size adjusted

Cause: VDISK changed the sector-size specification in the DEVICE=VDISK.SYS line in the CONFIG.SYS file.

Response: No response required.

Sector size too large in file *filename*

Cause: You specified a device driver that uses a sector size larger than the size defined for DOS.

Response: Change the sector size, so that it matches that of DOS. If the program is purchased software, return it to the dealer.

Seek error

Cause: DOS could not find a track on the disk.

Response: Reinsert the diskette, use another drive, or run CHKDSK.

Sharing Violation

Cause: One of two things has happened: you may have used an invalid sharing mode while trying to access a file. This error usually occurs when someone else is waiting to access the same file in compatibility mode or in sharing mode and so prevents you from using the file concurrently. Or, a file that XCOPY is trying to access is currently locked by another user.

Response: Reexecute processing or abort the SHARE command and enter it again later; wait until the file is available (after a few moments, typically) and reexecute XCOPY.

Source does not contain backup files

Cause: The source disk does not contain any backup files to be restored.

Response: No response required.

Source path required

Cause: You did not specify a path to the source of the replacement files.

Response: Reinvoke REPLACE specifying a source path.

Specified COMMAND search directory bad

Cause: You specified an invalid path.

Response: Reissue the command with a valid path.

System files restored
The target disk may not be bootable

Cause: During the restore process, the files IBMBIO.COM and IBMDOS.COM were restored.

If these files are from a previous version of DOS, your disk may not be bootable.

Response: Use SYS to transfer the correct version of the files to the disk from your master copy. You can use VER to help determine the DOS version numbers involved.

System transferred

Cause: The two hidden system files have been transferred to the newly formatted disk, an operation that occurs when you specify the /S parameter.

Response: No response required.

System will now restart
Insert DOS diskette in drive A:
Press any key when ready

Cause: To install the new partition information, the system must be rebooted.

Response: Insert a DOS diskette in drive A and reboot the system.

Target cannot be used for backup

Cause: An error occurred during writing to the destination disk.

Response: Use another disk. If the error recurs, restart the system or use another device as the backup operation target.

The last file was not restored

Cause: You interrupted the restore process in the middle of the last restoration; or the target disk ran out of room, and the last file, which was partially restored, was deleted.

Response: If you ran out of room, make room on the disk and continue the restore process from where you left off. If you stopped the process, reissue RESTORE for the files that have not been restored yet.

The only startable partition on Drive 1 is already set active

Cause: You have only one partition on the drive, and it is the active, boot partition.

Response: No response required.

Too many drive entries

Cause: You specified too many drive identifiers on the command line.

Response: Reissue the command with fewer drive identifiers.

Too many extent entries

Cause: You specified too many cache buffers (second parameter). All second parameter values must add up to less than 999.

Response: Reissue FASTOPEN with reduced extent (cache) entry values.

Too many open files

Cause: Insufficient file handles are available for use.

Response: Increase the FILES= command line in the CONFIG.SYS file to at least 20.

Total disk space is *x* Mbytes

Cause: This message displays the total available space on the hard disk.

Response: No response required.

Unable to create directory

Cause: One of the following errors occurred: The directory you are trying to create already exists; you specified an invalid directory on the path; the root directory is full; a file in the specified parent directory already exists by the name you want to use; you specified an invalid directory name.

Response: Verify that you entered a valid directory name and path and that no file already exists with the name you wish to use.

Unable to write BOOT

Cause: The boot record could not be written on the disk, because of a defective first track.

Response: Replace your hard disk.

Unrecoverable error in directory

Cause: CHKDSK found an error while examining a directory.

Response: No response required.

VERIFY is on | off

Cause: This message displays the current status of VERIFY.

Response: No response required.

Volume label (11 characters, ENTER for none)?

Cause: FORMAT asks you to enter a one to eleven-character volume label for the current disk.

Response: Enter a label; then press Enter.

WARNING! ALL DATA ON NON-REMOVABLE DISK DRIVE *X* WILL BE LOST
Proceed with Format (Y/N)?

Cause: FORMAT requests confirmation that you wish to format the specified hard disk.

Response: Type Y to format or N not to format the hard disk.

Warning—directory full
***x* file(s) recovered**

Cause: There is not enough space left on the disk to recover more files.

Response: Free sufficient space and rerun RECOVER.

Warning! Diskette is out of sequence
Replace the diskette or continue if okay
Strike any key when ready

Cause: You inserted the wrong disk for restoration.

Response: Use the correct diskette.

Warning! File *x*
is a read-only file
Replace the file (Y/N)?

Cause: The file indicated is a read-only file, and hence cannot be automatically overwritten.

Response: Enter Y to overwrite the file or N not to overwrite the file.

Warning! File *x*
was changed after it was backed up
Replace the file (Y/N)?

Cause: The file to be restored is an earlier version of one that already exists on the disk.

Response: Enter Y to replace the latest version with the earlier version or N to abort the replacement operation.

Warning! Files in the target drive
***d*:\BACKUP directory will be erased**
Press any key when ready

Cause: This warning appears when you issue the BACKUP command using a subdirectory as the target.

Response: Press Ctrl-Break to halt execution if you do not wish to continue; press any key to continue.

Warning! Files in the target drive
***d*:\root directory will be erased**
Strike any key when ready

Cause: This warning appears when you issue the BACKUP command using a diskette drive as the target.

Response: Press Ctrl-Break to halt execution if you do not wish to continue; press any key to continue.

Warning! No files were found to back up

Cause: DOS found no files to back up that matched your specification.

Response: Make sure you specified the desired file names correctly.

Warning! No files were found to restore

Response: Make sure you specified the desired file names correctly.

Warning! The partition set active is not startable

Cause: You have marked an unbootable partition as active.

Response: Change the active partition to one that is bootable.

APPENDIX C

Typical Hard Disk System Problems and Their Cures

This appendix describes some common problems you might confront while using your hard disk and suggests some possible courses of action to remedy these problems. This appendix does not list individual errors for which DOS provides messages (see Appendix B for that information), but rather describes general types of problems, their causes, and solutions. The intention here is to help you have a feeling for the probable causes of different classes of problems. You should then be able to identify the nature of a problem and, therefore, solve that problem more rapidly.

DOS File Manipulation Failures

System failures are not always due to hardware problems or software conflicts. Sometimes they are the result of a user input error—your error. This section discusses the possible errors in manipulating files that you might make in command or parameter entry.

Problem: Command works overall, but the files affected were not the intended files, or the selected files were not processed in the expected way.

Cause: Wildcards were used improperly.

Cure: If anything past the * is ignored, use the ? wildcard.

Cause: You are in the wrong directory and have executed a file with the same name as the file you want, but which is configured differently.

Cure: Change to the correct directory.

Cause: You sequenced your PATH or APPEND specifications improperly.

Cure: Check the order of directories and respecify the command.

Cause: You forgot to include a parameter.

Cure: Reenter the command, including the missing parameter.

Cause: You included an extra parameter.

Cure: Reenter the command, eliminating the extra parameter.

Problem: The command executed in an unexpected manner.

Cause: Another file of the same name but with a different extension was executed; for instance, you may have tried to execute TEST.BAT by typing TEST, but executed TEST.EXE instead. This problem can occur among .COM, .BAT, and .EXE files, because they can all be executed without specifying their extensions.

Cure: Specify the file extension in the command or check and revise the current and PATH directories.

Cause: Another file of the same name with or without the same extension was executed due to the sequence of the PATH or APPEND specification.

Cure: Resequence the PATH or APPEND setting, so that the directory containing the desired file comes before the directory containing the file you do *not* want executed. Remember that the directories specified by PATH and APPEND are searched sequentially from beginning to end.

Cause: You typed the wrong command name, such as DISKCOMP instead of DISKCOPY or instead of COMP.

Cure: Type the correct command name.

Problem: A command scrambles the display, locks the system, or generates a parity error.

Cause: The command is not compatible with memory-resident programs.

Cure: To identify the problem program, remove memory-resident programs one by one until the system works properly again. Do this by successively rebooting the system and loading all but one of the formerly loaded programs. Then reexecute the command or program that didn't work before to see if it works with the remaining TSRs.

Cause: The command file became scrambled. Sometimes, data saved on the disk can become scrambled.

Cure: Recopy or reenter the program and reexecute processing.

Cause: The disk is bad. The disk surface may be damaged.

Cure: Use CHKDSK to determine whether a media problem exists. If there is a problem, recopy the data onto another diskette, or have your hard disk serviced if you cannot rectify the problem using available software.

Cause: The program is configured for a different screen.

Cure: Check the user's manual for the device and verify that the configuration of your program is appropriate for your peripheral hardware. Especially check the screen and printer device drivers and types.

Disk Access Problems

Disks are central to much of your computer use. You store your files on them, you obtain new software on them, you back up data to them, you access them constantly over the course of a typical computer session. You can significantly reduce frustration by learning how to handle the range of possible disk problems discussed in this section.

Problem: When you try to access the disk, it does not stop, you cannot hear or feel any head movement, and the display is not being updated to tell you that the computer is actually accomplishing anything.

Cause: The specified path contains numerous directories, or the amount of data being loaded is very large.

Cure: If a blinking message telling you to wait appears, processing is underway. However, unless the current program explicitly asks you to wait, you should not need to wait more than a minute or so for something to happen without an indicator appearing on the screen. If there is any doubt about what the program is doing, consult someone knowledgeable or the documentation.

Problem: Inconsistent disk failures occur: The screen displays many error messages, which may not always

be the same; your programs don't work; or the system locks.

Cause: Poor ventilation and extra circuit cards inside of the computer can combine to make the interior of the system unit excessively warm. Heat causes chips and circuitry to malfunction.

Cure: Verify that the fan is working. Verify that the ventilation holes, both for air intake and expulsion, are unobstructed. Feel the back of the unit to see if it is excessively warm; you may need a more powerful fan or power supply. If you cannot remedy the problem yourself, see your dealer or maintenance department.

Cause: Media problems occur: The disk may be storing information on parts of the disk that the computer does not know are bad, and hence, the data is subject to error.

Cure: Recopy your programs or data to another area of the disk and use that file. Leave the bad data on the disk, so that the computer will not again use that area of the disk. If you have any diagnostic programs, use these to test for errors. The Disk Test utility in the Norton Utilities (see Chapter 3) will not only check for disk problems, but will mark bad clusters, so they won't be reused for later file storage. Also, use CHKDSK to see if it can find any errors.

Cause: You are on a network, and lockup-prevention software is not available or not working correctly.

Cure: If you do not have lockup-prevention software, contact your network dealer. If you do have this type of software, and it is not working correctly, make a new copy of your NETBIOS or other support programs. If the problem recurs, consult your dealer.

Problem: The wrong directory is displayed or the wrong disk is accessed.

Cause: You are running a program in another directory by using PATH and APPEND.

Cure: If directory paths are not supported by the program, you must exit the program and execute it from the directory containing the desired program. If directory paths are supported, consult your application software user's manuals to determine how to specify which directory should be displayed.

Cause: You did not specify the drive you wanted.

Cure: Specify the correct drive.

Cause: You did not *correctly* specify the drive you wanted.

Cure: Specify the drive correctly.

Cause: You are not in the directory you think you are in.

Cure: Check the directory name to determine the current directory.

Problem: Much abnormal noise and/or use of the drive. The drive takes a long time to access data.

Cause: A media problem exists.

Cure: Copy as much of your disk as you can onto a new diskette and use that instead.

Cause: Your program is very fragmented. Programs and data may not be stored sequentially on the hard disk, resulting in much head movement, which causes noise.

Cure: Buy a disk optimization program, such as the Norton Utilities (see Chapter 3) or VOPT, to eliminate file fragmentation.

Problem: The disk is not activated when it is being accessed, and the operation fails or the computer locks.

Cause: Your system has heat-dissipation problems.

Cure: Verify that the fan is working. Verify that the ventilation holes, both for air intake and expulsion, are unobstructed. Feel the back of the unit to see if it is excessively warm; you may need a more powerful fan or power supply. If you cannot remedy the problem yourself, see your dealer or maintenance department.

Cause: Your disk controller has problems.

Cure: Run CHKDSK along with any other diagnostic programs you have. Turn off the computer and reboot. If the problem recurs, contact your dealer.

Cause: Resident program interaction problems exists.

Cure: To identify the problem program, remove memory-resident programs one by one until the system works properly again. Do this by successively rebooting the system and loading all but one of the formerly loaded programs. Then reexecute the command or program that didn't work before to see if it works with the remaining TSRs.

APPENDIX D

Partitioning Your Hard Disk

Hard disks are usually so large that they can contain more than one type of operating system. For example, you can have DOS manage one part of a disk and UNIX manage another. Each of these sections is called a *partition*. You can have from one to four partitions on a disk.

Partitions are used to make the hard disk, especially a very large one, a more economical investment. They allow you to have, in effect, up to four completely different computer systems resident in one set of hardware. However, since they do not share a common software environment, they cannot share data directly.

Two types of partitions can be set up for DOS: a primary DOS partition and, beginning with DOS 3.3, an extended DOS partition. The primary DOS partition contains DOS itself and is the first partition on the disk. It is the only partition on a typical user's hard disk, especially if that disk is no larger than 32Mb. DOS 4 can create partitions that are larger than 32Mb; this was the maximum partition size in DOS versions 3.3 and earlier.

The extended DOS partition is a separate partition that cannot be used for booting, but can be divided into separate logical drives. This is convenient for preparing logically separate disk drives out of one very large physical drive. If you are using a backup medium that is limited to 16Mb (as are some tape drives) or 20Mb (as are some removable hard-disk cartridges), the backup process is simplified if you can back up an entire logical drive onto the backup device with one command.

If you have chosen to create an extended DOS partition, it is assigned the next logical drive letter. For example, if you had a 60Mb hard-disk drive, you could create a 30Mb primary partition and a 30Mb extended partition. The primary partition could be accessed as drive C, while the extended partition would be called drive D. You could also subdivide the extended partition into more logical drives (up to the letter Z).

You must create partitions before using a hard-disk drive. Most users take the easiest route, simply making the entire disk into one primary partition. The FDISK program presented here, however, is also necessary in several more advanced situations. For example, you may plan on using multiple operating systems from the same disk. FDISK will let you set up unique partitions for each system. (Each of these would be a primary partition, but only one could be designated the active partition, the one that will gain control at start-up.)

Then again, you may be using one of the large hard disks (70Mb and up) that are increasingly common. With DOS 4, you can create one partition for the entire space, but, as suggested earlier, you may do better by partitioning the larger physical drive into multiple logical drives.

> ***Caution:*** *FDISK assigns drive letters to the primary partitions of all physical drives before assigning any letters to logical drives in any extended partitions.*

Occasionally, you may install a second hard-disk drive on your DOS system. When you do this and use FDISK to prepare the required disk partitions, you should understand how FDISK assigns drive identifier letters. The primary partition of the second hard disk becomes drive D, and all drive identifiers of any logical drives in the first disk's extended partition will be bumped up by one letter. For example, if your first disk had a primary drive C and an extended partition drive D, adding a second hard drive would make the former drive D into a new drive E (since the new physical hard drive's primary partition will now become drive D).

Throughout all of this required partitioning processing, you must be careful not to lose any existing data on your hard disk. If your disk is already being used and you wish to make a new partition, you will have to first back up all of your data and then run FDISK from a system disk. Then, you'll need to reformat your disk before restoring your files to it.

Configuring a DOS Partition

In this section, you will learn exactly how to use the FDISK command. This procedure is very important, and it can have serious consequences if done incorrectly. However, when done properly, it can make your system more efficient.

If you are using a DOS version earlier than 4.0, your screen displays will differ slightly from those shown here, but the steps to follow are almost exactly the same. Such minor differences as occur are noted throughout this discussion.

> ***Caution:*** *Any existing data on your disk will be destroyed when you create partitions with FDISK.*

The FDISK command requires no arguments, and can be easily invoked from the File System window of DOS 4 or by typing **FDISK** and pressing ↵. After this command creates the appropriate partition(s), you must then logically format the disk(s). Any existing data on your disk(s) will be destroyed when you create partitions with FDISK.

When you first execute FDISK, the screen will clear and the FDISK Options screen shown in Figure D.1 will appear. This contains the menu used to get around in FDISK. As you can see, there are four choices. (Options 1 and 3 in version 3.3 do not refer explicitly to logical DOS drives, but they are also used for that purpose.) If you have a system with more than one hard-disk drive, the number in the *Current fixed disk drive: 1* line would be changed to reflect the drive being partitioned. Also, a fifth option, *Select next fixed disk drive*, would be displayed on the screen. You can work on only one hard-disk drive at a time, but you can switch from the drive you are working on to another drive. For now, let's assume you have one hard-disk drive and that you'll receive the four choices shown.

```
                    IBM DOS Version 4.00
                  Fixed Disk Setup Program
              (C)Copyright IBM Corp. 1983, 1988

                        FDISK Options

Current fixed disk drive: 1

Choose one of the following:

1. Create DOS Partition or Logical DOS Drive
2. Set active partition
3. Delete DOS Partition or Logical DOS Drive
4. Display partition information


Enter choice: [1]




Press Esc to exit FDISK
```

Figure D.1: The main FDISK Options menu

Creating a Partition

The first option on the FDISK Options menu is to create a DOS partition. Since you are using DOS, and not another operating system like UNIX, you can only create DOS partitions. Should you wish to put another operating system onto the disk, that system would have its own partitioning command, equivalent to FDISK, which would create its partitions next to DOS's. Choosing the first option to create a DOS partition results in the Create DOS Partition screen shown in Figure D.2. In DOS 3.3, option 3 only appears after you have actually created an extended DOS partition.

> ***Tip:*** *If you plan to use your hard disk later to support another operating system, do not partition the whole disk. Leave some room, so that another system can be loaded onto the disk.*

Creating the Primary DOS Partition

Assuming you are starting from scratch, select choice 1 to create the primary DOS partition. You will then see the screen shown in Figure D.3.

```
              Create DOS Partition or Logical DOS Drive

Current fixed disk drive: 1

Choose one of the following:

1. Create Primary DOS Partition
2. Create Extended DOS Partition
3. Create Logical DOS Drive(s) in the Extended DOS Partition



Enter choice: [1]




Press Esc to return to FDISK Options
```

Figure D.2: The Create DOS Partition menu

```
                    Create Primary DOS Partition

Current fixed disk drive: 1

Do you wish to use the maximum available size for a Primary DOS Partition
and make the partition active (Y/N)....................? [Y]









Press Esc to return to FDISK Options
```

Figure D.3: Creating the primary DOS partition

If you want to use the whole disk for the primary DOS partition, answer Y on this screen. Doing so makes DOS use the whole disk. The computer will allocate the entire disk, and then come back with this message:

> **System will now restart**
> **Insert DOS Install diskette in drive A:**
> **Press any key when ready . . .**

Since you just created the partition, there is now nothing on the hard disk. The system must be rebooted from a floppy disk, either the Install diskette that is one of your original DOS diskettes or one you have formatted with the /S switch. You can now format the entire hard disk just as you would a floppy disk.

On the other hand, if you answer N, you'll have the opportunity to create a smaller partition. You would then receive a screen similar to that seen in Figure D.4.

There are only two reasons not to accept the entire physical disk space for your primary DOS partition. First, you may want to reserve some space on the disk for another operating system. Second, you may want to create additional logical drives for use by DOS. As Figure D.4 shows, in DOS 4 you can define your primary DOS partition in either absolute numbers of megabytes or in a percentage of total disk space. Your entry is interpreted as a number of megabytes if you simply enter a number, or as a percentage of total physical disk space if you follow the number with a percent sign. In earlier versions of DOS, you define the partition size in numbers of cylinders.

The example disk being partitioned in this demonstrative sequence has a total of 41 megabytes (nominally a 40Mb hard disk).

```
                    Create Primary DOS Partition
Current fixed disk drive: 1



Total disk space is   41 Mbytes (1 Mbyte = 1048576 bytes)
Maximum space available for partition is   41 Mbytes (100%)

Enter partition size in Mbytes or percent of disk space (%) to
create a Primary DOS Partition.................................: [  20]

No partitions defined

Press Esc to return to FDISK Options
```

Figure D.4: Specifying the size of the primary DOS partition

The partition size shown in Figure E.4 has been entered as an absolute number of 20Mb.

The message near the bottom of the screen, *No partitions defined*, reflects only the fact that you have not yet created any disk partitions. That's what you're about to do. Pressing ↵ creates the primary DOS partition and produces the status screen shown in Figure D.5.

This screen tells you that the partition you just created on drive C is a primary DOS partition (PRI DOS) that is 20 megabytes large, constituting 49% of the entire physical disk. (In DOS version 3.3 you'll see the number of cylinders, and their starting and ending points, but not the percentage of total disk space.) The *Status* item indicates whether the partition is active. At this point it is not, so the field is blank. Pressing Esc at this point returns you to the FDISK Options menu.

> ***Note:*** *There can be only one primary DOS partition. When DOS boots up, the system files from this partition are loaded into memory for your operations.*

At this point, you could select choice 2 on the main menu to activate this particular primary partition (PRI DOS). It will then be used for booting your system at power up time.

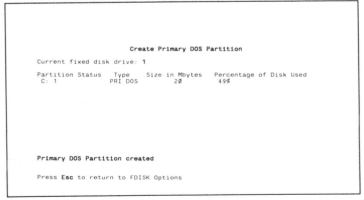

```
                    Create Primary DOS Partition

Current fixed disk drive: 1

Partition Status   Type    Size in Mbytes   Percentage of Disk Used
 C: 1             PRI DOS        20             49%




Primary DOS Partition created

Press Esc to return to FDISK Options
```

Figure D.5: Primary DOS partition is created

Creating an Extended DOS Partition (Versions 3.3 and 4 Only)

In this example, you have only used 20 megabytes out of a possible 41, so you can now take one of two further stops. You can install another operating system in the remaining space, or (in versions 3.3 and higher) create an extended DOS partition and define logical DOS disks in that space. That's what you'll do now. To do so, you select choice 1 on the FDISK Options menu (see Figure D.1) and then select choice 2 on the Create menu (see Figure D.2).

The resulting screen (see Figure D.6) allows you to create an extended DOS partition. This screen tells you the current partitioning status: there is a maximum available space of 21Mb, or 51% of the available physical disk. (Again, in version 3.3 the space is measured in cylinders.) This value of 21 is displayed as the default entry here for the extended DOS partition size. You need only enter a number over the default to override that value. In Figure D.6, 51% was entered for the desired extended DOS partition, leaving no remaining space on this disk for another operating system.

Press ↵, and the screen will now clear, redisplaying the new disk partition information, including that on the new extended DOS partition (see Figure D.7).

```
                    Create Extended DOS Partition

Current fixed disk drive: 1

Partition Status   Type    Size in Mbytes   Percentage of Disk Used
 C: 1       A     PRI DOS        20              49%



Total disk space is   41 Mbytes (1 Mbyte = 1048576 bytes)
Maximum space available for partition is   21 Mbytes ( 51%)

Enter partition size in Mbytes or percent of disk space (%) to
create an Extended DOS Partition.............................: [ 51%]



Press Esc to return to FDISK Options
```

Figure D.6: Creating an extended DOS partition

Pressing Esc enables you to continue with the the next step of the process. In version 4, you can now return to the screen of Figure E.2 to create logical drives within the now existing extended partition. If you select choice 3 on the Create DOS Partition screen now, DOS tells you that no logical drives have yet been defined in this extended partition (see Figure D.8). You are also shown the size of the extended partition and the amount available for defining logical

```
                    Create Extended DOS Partition

Current fixed disk drive: 1

Partition Status   Type    Size in Mbytes   Percentage of Disk Used
 C: 1        A     PRI DOS        20             49%
    2              EXT DOS        21             51%



Extended DOS Partition created

Press Esc to continue
```

Figure D.7: Extended DOS partition creation screen

```
        Create Logical DOS Drive(s) in the Extended DOS Partition


No logical drives defined


Total Extended DOS Partition size is   21 Mbytes (1 MByte = 1048576 bytes)
Maximum space available for logical drive is   21 Mbytes (100%)

Enter logical drive size in Mbytes or percent of disk space (%)...[  15]


Press Esc to return to FDISK Options
```

Figure D.8: Creating logical drive D in an extended partition

drives. Because no other logical drives have been defined yet, the entire extended partition is available. Your entry on this screen will define the size of the first logical drive. This will become drive D, since the primary DOS partition is assigned the drive identifier C. Let's say you enter 15 (or a comparable number of cylinders). This creates logical drive D, representing an assignment of 72% of the available 21Mb in this extended partition. Because all available space in the extended partition has not been used, the resulting screen, shown in Figure D.9, enables you immediately to assign the remaining 6Mb (28%).

You could simply press ↵ to accept the assignment of this remaining 6Mb to another logical DOS drive (E). The resulting screen, shown in Figure D.10, contains the logical drive information, consisting of both identifying and sizing information.

Setting or Changing the Active Partition

The *active* partition is that partition that is used to boot the system. It is the default partition. Choosing option 2 on the main

```
            Create Logical DOS Drive(s) in the Extended DOS Partition

Drv Volume Label  Mbytes  System   Usage
D:                    15  UNKNOWN    72%





     Total Extended DOS Partition size is   21 Mbytes (1 MByte = 1048576 bytes)
     Maximum space available for logical drive is    6 Mbytes ( 28%)

     Enter logical drive size in Mbytes or percent of disk space (%)...[   6]

     Logical DOS Drive created, drive letters changed or added

     Press Esc to return to FDISK Options
```

Figure D.9: Creating logical drive E in an extended partition

FDISK Options menu leads you to a screen like that shown in Figure D.11, in which the partition information is displayed. This particular screen represents the partition status as it existed before the extended partition was created. FDISK now wants to know the number of the partition that you wish to make active.

```
            Create Logical DOS Drive(s) in the Extended DOS Partition

Drv Volume Label  Mbytes  System   Usage
D:                    15  UNKNOWN    72%
E:                     6  UNKNOWN    28%










     All available space in the Extended DOS Partition
     is assigned to logical drives.
     Press Esc to return to FDISK Options
```

Figure D.10: Final logical DOS drive creation screen

```
                         Set Active Partition

     Current fixed disk drive: 1

     Partition Status    Type     Size in Mbytes   Percentage of Disk Used
      C: 1              PRI DOS          2Ø           49%


     Total disk space is   41 Mbytes (1 Mbyte = 1Ø48576 bytes)

     Enter the number of the partition you want to make active...........: [1]




     Press Esc to return to FDISK Options
```

Figure D.11: The Set Active Partition screen

Typically, you type the number 1, so that the primary DOS partition will have control when the system comes up. However, if you have partitioned your disk to include another operating system, choice 2 allows you to activate that operating system the next time the hard disk boots up. You cannot start the system from an extended DOS partition, because the necessary startup files are located in the primary partition, and DOS will display an error message to this effect if you attempt to do so. Entering the desired valid partition number and pressing ↵ will result in a message that your selected partition has been made active.

Displaying Partition Information

Option 4 on the FDISK Options menu is used to display information about the partitions. This is useful because no extra functions will be executed at the same time; you can simply look at the information. In DOS 4, choosing option 4 yields the screen shown in Figure D.12. (Earlier DOS versions, as usual, display the size information measured in cylinders.)

To see information about the logical drives that have been defined, respond Y to the prompt asking if you want to see this information. You'll see a screen like that shown in Figure D.13.

```
                        Display Partition Information

Current fixed disk drive: 1

Partition Status   Type     Size in Mbytes   Percentage of Disk Used
 C: 1        A    PRI DOS        20            49%
    2             EXT DOS        21            51%


Total disk space is   41 Mbytes (1 Mbyte = 1048576 bytes)

The Extended DOS Partition contains Logical DOS Drives.
Do you want to display the logical drive information (Y/N)......?[Y]



Press Esc to return to FDISK Options
```

Figure D.12: Displaying partition information

Deleting DOS Partitions

As with most things, what DOS giveth, DOS can taketh away, with a little prodding from you. Selecting choice 3 on the FDISK Options menu produces the Delete DOS Partition menu, shown in Figure D.14. In earlier versions of DOS, only the title of this screen changes to include reference to logical DOS drives. The subsequent three choices are precisely the same.

```
                    Display Logical DOS Drive Information

Drv Volume Label  Mbytes  System   Usage
D:                    15  UNKNOWN    72%
E:                     6  UNKNOWN    28%



    Total Extended DOS Partition size is   21 Mbytes (1 MByte = 1048576 bytes)



    Press Esc to return to FDISK Options
```

Figure D.13: Displaying logical DOS drive information

```
                 Delete DOS Partition or Logical DOS Drive

    Current fixed disk drive: 1

    Choose one of the following:

    1.  Delete Primary DOS Partition
    2.  Delete Extended DOS Partition
    3.  Delete Logical DOS Drive(s) in the Extended DOS Partition


    Enter choice: [ ]



    Press Esc to return to FDISK Options
```

Figure D.14: The Delete DOS Partition menu

Using this menu, you can delete any of the information you've already set up. You may want to expand or contract other partitions, or you may no longer want to use a partition in the manner you originally designed. In any case, you can make changes only in a certain order. You cannot delete the primary DOS partition without first deleting the extended DOS partition.

In addition, you cannot delete an extended DOS partition without first deleting the logical drives in that partition. Trying to delete the extended DOS partition before deleting the drives in it will simply display the current partition information with a message informing you that FDISK can't perform the required deletion.

Choice 3 in the Delete DOS Partition menu is probably the first selection you will need to make; you work your way backward in the order in which you created things. Actually, you will find that this is a fairly natural process. Selecting choice 3 produces a screen that contains the logical drive information and the size of the extended DOS partition that contains the drives. As before, this information is displayed in megabytes for DOS 4 users, and in a cylinder range for DOS 3.3 users. You are also warned that any data contained in the logical disk drive to be deleted will also be deleted (lost). If necessary, take this opportunity to abort the FDISK program and copy any files you want to preserve to another disk.

If you still want to delete the drive, simply enter the drive identifier. You will then be asked to enter the logical drive's volume label if it has one. You must enter the correct label; otherwise FDISK will not delete the logical drive. If it has no volume label, simply pressing ↵ is sufficient here. Furthermore, you will then be asked to confirm this step explicitly. You will enter Y to do this. If you enter N, you are returned to the FDISK Options menu.

Figure D.15 displays the deletion sequence just described for a disk that had a 9Mb extended DOS partition consisting of drive D. DOS 4 users must know and enter the volume label of the drive to proceed; DOS 3.3 users are at somewhat greater risk of deleting the wrong material, since this protective question is not included for them. Once FDISK deletes the logical drive, it updates the display at the top of the screen. If you have any remaining logical drives in your extended partition, FDISK asks for another drive to delete. You would then follow the same procedure to delete other drives.

When the last logical drive is deleted, the display indicates the drive identifiers that have been deleted and informs you that

All logical drives deleted in the Extended DOS Partition

Pressing Esc at this point will bring you back to the main FDISK Options menu. Now that the logical drives are gone, you can delete the extended DOS partition itself if you choose to do so. Choosing option 2 on the Delete DOS Partition menu results in the by-now familiar screen that shows the partition information display, warning that data will be lost and asking if you really want to delete the extended DOS partition. If you reply Y, the screen will be updated to show only the primary DOS partition and a message that the extended DOS partition has been deleted. Press Esc to return once again to the FDISK Options menu.

```
          Delete Logical DOS Drive(s) in the Extended DOS Partition

Drv Volume Label  Mbytes  System   Usage
D:                     9  UNKNOWN   100%





    Total Extended DOS Partition size is      9 Mbytes (1 MByte = 1048576 bytes)

    WARNING! Data in a deleted Logical DOS Drive will be lost.
    What drive do you want to delete..............................? [D]
    Enter Volume Label............................? [           ]
    Are you sure (Y/N)............................? [Y]

    Press Esc to return to FDISK Options
```

Figure D.15: Deleting logical DOS drives

Index

Note: *Italic* page numbers refer to information presented in tables.

Hard Disk DOS Learning Aids

If you have found this Instant Reference to be useful, you'll be glad to learn that Judd Robbins has produced a number of useful DOS learning aids. All of the batch files in his two DOS books, *Mastering DOS* and the *DOS User's Desktop Companion*, are available on a special Companion Diskette. Save time, energy, and money—and avoid the drudgery of typing these excellent programs—by ordering the *DOS Companion Diskette* now.

If you have friends or colleagues who would like to begin learning DOS at an elementary level, you should try the *Introduction to DOS Audio Cassette Training* program. This introductory training guide contains two audio cassettes and an accompanying "Professional Learning Manual" with exercises and learning modules that parallel the tapes. Send in your order for this personal aid to quick and easy understanding of DOS.

Use the order form below to order any of the fine DOS products produced by Judd Robbins. Mail the form with complete payment to Computer Options, 198 Amherst Avenue, Berkeley, CA 94708. Please specify desired disk format (5¼" or 3½"). If not specified, 5¼" diskettes will be sent.

______ copies of *DOS Companion Diskette* @ $19.95 each = ______
___ 5¼"format OR ___ 3½" format

______ copies of *Introduction to DOS Audio Cassette Training* program @ $19.95 each = ______

______ copies of *ReComm*, the DOS Command Reissuing utility @ $19.95 each = ______
___ 5¼" format OR ___ 3½" format

Shipping and handling @ $2.50/product ______

California sales tax (California residents only; add appropriate tax for your city or county) ______

TOTAL ORDER: ______

NAME: ______________________________

COMPANY: ______________________________

ADDRESS: ______________________________

CITY, STATE, ZIP: ______________________________

TELEPHONE: ______________________________

SYBEX *is not affiliated with* Computer Options *and assumes no responsibility for any defect in the disks, programs, or training materials.*